MW00795662

מאמר
לא תהי' משכלה
תשי"ב

FULL DEVOTION

מאמר
לא תהי' משכלה
תשי"ב

FULL DEVOTION

a chasidic discourse by
The Lubavitcher Rebbe
Rabbi Menachem M. Schneerson
זצוקללה"ה נבג"מ זי"ע

•

translated by
Rabbi Zalman Abraham

Kehot Publication Society
770 Eastern Parkway / Brooklyn, New York 11213

Full Devotion

Kehot Publication Society
770 Eastern Parkway / Brooklyn, New York 11213
(718) 774-4000 / Fax (718) 774-2718
editor@kehot.com

Orders:
291 Kingston Avenue / Brooklyn, New York 11213
(718) 778-0226 / Fax (718) 778-4148
www.kehot.com

ISBN: 978-0-8266-0751-5

Manufactured in the United States of America

CONTENTS

ב"ה

PREFACE

We are pleased to present *Full Devotion*, an English translation of a discourse delivered by the Lubavitcher Rebbe, Rabbi Menachem M. Schneerson, of blessed memory, on Shabbat Parashat Mishpatim, 5712 (1952).

The discourse, which opens with the verse (Exodus 23:26) *None shall miscarry or be barren in your land; the number of your days I will fill*, has been referred to as a landmark discourse, delivered by the Rebbe barely two years after ascending to the leadership of Chabad-Lubavitch. The discourse is perhaps unique among all of the Rebbe's teachings in the sense that its message required a retooling of our conception of divine service. It discusses the self-satisfaction that might result from our love and awe of G-d, and that contemplating the fact that our days upon Earth need to be utilized to the fullest serves to remove any such feelings of satisfaction.

At one point during its 55-minute delivery, the Rebbe broke down weeping and rested his head on the table for a short while.

Even without having been present, the reader can sense the immeasurable devotion emanating from the mind and heart of a true servant of G-d, as he charges us with the task of continuously choosing to look beyond ourselves, with *Full Devotion*, to see G-d's love for us, which in turn, will make us successful in loving and serving Him.

* * *

It is important to bear in mind that this discourse was delivered on a Shabbat, in Yiddish, and was transcribed in Hebrew, after Shabbat's end, by the students of the central Lubavitch Yeshiva based on their oral review. It has never been formally edited for publication by the Rebbe[1] and is part of

1. Apart from a section published in *Likkutei Sichot*, vol. 16, pp. 271-274.

the "unedited" genre of Chasidic discourses. Thus, any possible inaccuracies are due to the above, and the Rebbe's precise expressions and nuances may be lost in the transcript. The Hebrew text appearing in the present work is reproduced from *Torat Menachem – Hitvaaduyot,* vol. 4, p. 323 ff.

* * *

The discourse was translated and annotated by Rabbi Zalman Abraham. Special thanks are due to Rabbi Shmuel Klatzkin for writing the introduction, to Rabbi Avraham D. Vaisfiche for reviewing the text and annotations, to Rabbis Yosef B. Friedman and Dovid Olidort for their editorial guidance, and to Rabbi Mendel Laine for coordinating the project.

Kehot Publication Society

28 Sivan 5770
Brooklyn, New York

THE LUBAVITCHER REBBE
RABBI MENACHEM MENDEL SCHNEERSON
זצוקללה״ה נבג״מ זי״ע

INTRODUCTION

INTRODUCTION

At a Chassidic gathering in the winter of 5712 (1952), the Lubavitcher Rebbe led those present into an exploration of the nature of G-d's blessings. His talk centered on these verses from the book of Exodus, appearing in the Torah portion of that week, *Mishpatim*:

> And you shall serve the L-rd your G-d and He shall bless your bread and your water and I will remove sickness from your midst. None shall miscarry or be barren in your land; the number of your days I will fill (Exodus 23: 25-26).

It is very basic that we seek G-d's blessing. In our human condition, we must constantly act with limited information and limited power, even on those issues most important in our lives. How natural, then, to ask the One whose knowledge and whose power is sufficient to grant us what it is that we need.

The text offers a blessing from G-d in three fundamental areas of our human need: food, health and progeny. But the blessings are not framed by G-d as a giveaway, but as His response to our commitment to His service.

It seems intuitively right that G-d would not like us to be beggars, that His blessings should come within a relationship in which we offer something meaningful in return for what we receive. But what can we offer that means anything to G-d?

Here is a question that lies at the heart of religious life. What does our life mean to G-d? What can we offer Him? Without needing too much sophistication, we realize that we are dependent on G-d for everything, even our very existence. On the other hand, we know that G-d is absolutely independent in every respect, owing no aspect of His existence to any other being. In what way does our service mean anything to Him?

The Rebbe follows some classic insight, quoting the teachings of a great mystical work, *Avodat Hakodesh*, that service of G-d only relates to G-d as He has involved Himself in the world.

The idea is this: We sense that there is G-dliness within the world. We get an insight here, an inspiration there. Yet the more we are self-aware, the more we know that as G-dly as our insights are, they're necessarily limited. We are only grasping an aspect of G-dliness that is capable of being contained by our grasp.

Almost paradoxically, this insight that our grasp is limited frees us. We are free of pretense about our own grasp. We no longer have to believe that the limited concept our soul has grasped is the whole G-d whom we worship. Accordingly, we are free from serving our own concepts and we can turn with a whole heart towards G-d Himself, expanding our mind, transcending our limits.

If we were to accept our own grasp as giving the final word, we would get nothing done in regard to serving G-d. We therefore need to set these limits aside, turn away from serving our own idea of our own perfect grasp, and thus become free to devote ourselves more fully to G-d's service. Our service of G-d may not be perfect, but it is meaningful. We will not halt prematurely, transfixed with ourselves, looking in a mirror instead of towards G-d. And as we devote ourselves to serving G-d, and do not content ourselves with making an idol of the insights we have managed to grasp, we actually are relating to G-d. As a result of such service, we will be raising ourselves up, climbing the ladder of insight higher and higher.

But perhaps all such striving is still really only relating to our own limited grasp? If we go from a smaller to a larger grasp, are we not still only relating to our own grasp? What does it have to do, not with any particular level of reality that G-d has created, but with G-d Himself? The mystical text the Rebbe first quoted states that our service doesn't reach beyond the level of G-d's will, for the primordial delight-in-being that describes the essence from which will emerges is beyond our ability to relate to through service. To put it more simply—our service doesn't relate to G-d Himself, just to His creations. To G-d Himself, however, in His absolute independence, nothing makes a difference.

To find a way past this seeming impasse, the Rebbe turns to examine the language of the Torah itself in the verses quoted above. Who is speaking these words of the Torah?

In the words *And you shall serve the L-rd your G-d and He shall bless your bread and your water*, the speaker is a hidden third person. Moses isn't speaking; "the L-rd your G-d" isn't speaking—He is being spoken about. The significance of this simple phrase is that this teaching is coming from something above the name of G-d, from the essence above names—the utterly independent self of G-d, above all conceptualization and relation.

What this means is that our service of G-d is not a vain attempt on our own to relate to the Absolute that is always beyond us. Instead, we find that the Absolute will not be confined to infinity; neither are we isolated from Him because of our own intrinsic limitations. G-d's essence is truly ineffable and inconceivable, yet it is inviting our relation through service.

True, we cannot dare to say that we define G-d or limit Him through this or any other way of service. It is rather the *effect* of the service, the result of our response to G-d that means something. Just as in the love of another person, we learn to relate to that person as he is—the beloved is not just a concept of our brain or the concoction of our imagination; so, too, we learn to open ourselves to who G-d is rather than to reduce Him to our grasp.

What do we do when we accept service of G-d? We nullify our own will, our own understanding of self, before His will. By serving, we make a nothing of ourselves, and so enter that realm of "nothingness" which is G-d's alone—the pure absolute of His essence that is beyond any confines of "thingness."

Now, as the Rebbe continues to examine the verses, he points out how the voice suddenly switches to the first person: *I will remove sickness from your midst. None shall miscarry or be barren in your land; the number of your days I will fill.* That is, by shedding our own boundaries by entering G-d's service, we now hear a first-person voice addressing us—we hear the divine I, and it is bestowing blessings.

The blessings are then set by G-d as His response to the effect of our service. By stretching the bounds of our ego, by renouncing our habit of continuous self-reference so that we can engage entirely in the task of service, we have become a part of the relationship of blessing, and these blessings are now the nature of our lives. There will be sustenance in plenty. Sickness is removed, even if it has been present until now. There will be progeny, heirs to carry on the heritage of our lives.

These blessings as well reveal their G-dly nature in their deeper effect. Focusing on the last of the blessings, and following the Kabbalistic understanding that progeny refers to our emotions, the Rebbe teaches that the blessing is not just the physical surface, but also something far deeper and penetrating to the root of our own selves. To be precise, by our service, we make room within our minds and hearts to actually love G-d. The love will not just be our effort, and thus only a willful imagining of what love might be like, but the meeting of our selfless desire with G-d's own desire to be loved. From this union springs progeny—we are not barren, but blessed with offspring.

The service that elicits these blessings may begin in awe, our stance before the Infinite, but it is only fulfilled through love. Love, as the Rebbe describes it, is not an effortless falling, but a process that requires continuous choosing. One must make room for another, and this means one cannot be full of one's self. This is not a matter of being satisfied with our feelings, or with our apprehension of having achieved a certain worthy level. It requires a continuous emptying, a constant turning beyond ourselves, a making of room.

This brings us to the last part of this blessing, *The number of your days I will fill.* We should recall that our days on earth are numbered; we have been given a specific amount of time and specific talents and opportunities with which to fulfill our purpose in life. If we use these gifts for purposes other than fulfilling our unique mission—even good purposes—we thereby betray our divine charge. When, because of this realization, we are driven to fulfill our purpose on Earth, we become so involved in spreading light that we have no time to pause and wonder where we stand on the ladder of spiritual attainments. We become oblivious to our own spiritual status. And then, God indeed *fills the number of our days*—He takes those days in which we did not fulfill our purpose and makes them complete and radiant.

So the opening verse now reads, *There will be no miscarriage or barrenness caused by focusing on your own will if you contemplate the number of your days and allow Me to fill them.*

As the Rebbe speaks of this, he breaks down and cannot continue for a time. The emotions are deep and real; the Rebbe has been living all these ideas, not just theorizing. Even without having witnessed it, the reader can feel the Rebbe's open heart, teaching beyond the words how we all must put our own heart and soul on the line for the sake of divine service.

Thus, the message is:

Sometimes our knowledge cannot produce "offspring" because the heart is not receptive to the mind's message. Other times the heart is moved to feelings but they fail to produce a lasting transformation of the heart's nature—the love is not viable. Knowing of G-d's essential desire for that transformation, one should disdain all interest in personal experience and proclaim, "No love, no fear, no delight! G-d is waiting for our service!"

NOTE ON THE HEBREW TEXT: In vowelizing the Hebrew words in this edition we have followed the grammatical rules of the Holy Tongue, which occasionally differ from the traditional or colloquial pronunciation. The original footnotes by the publisher of the Hebrew text appear at the end of the *maamar*.

TRANSLATION AND COMMENTARY

With the help of Heaven, Shabbat Parashat Mishpatim, Parshat Shekalim, Mevarchim Hachodesh Adar, 5712

1.

None shall miscarry or be barren in your land; the number of your days I will fill.[1]

The verse prior to this one had stated: *And you shall serve the L-rd your G-d and He shall bless your bread and your water and I will remove illness from your midst.* It continues to relate that on account of this, also, *none shall miscarry*, and so on.[2]

CHILDREN, HEALTH, & LIVELIHOOD

This verse mentions a promise for the three [primary] blessings, the blessings of children, health *and* livelihood,[3] asserting that these blessings will come in tremendous abundance.

He shall bless your bread and your water is a blessing for livelihood. The verse states specifically, *and he shall **bless***, which means not only will there be enough livelihood, but there will be an additional blessing—abundant livelihood.

The verse continues, speaking about health in the same style, stating not only *And I will remove illness from your midst*, but moreover, *the number of your days I will fill*—a blessing for longevity.

Similarly, regarding the blessing for children the verse states, *None shall miscarry or be barren*. This refers to the blessing to bear children (the opposite of barrenness) and for their survival (the opposite of miscarriage). The blessing will also manifest itself in additional measure in the children's longevity even once the parents grow old (as we find regarding our patriarch Jacob, who when he thought that he had lost one of his children, he stated: "*If I be bereaved of my children* [sha-

1. Exodus 23:26.

2. The simple connection between the verses is that when the bread and water are blessed—i.e., the local water sources and produce carry no dis-

בס״ד. ש״פ משפטים, פרשת שקלים, מבה״ח אדר, ה׳תשי״ב

(הנחה בלתי מוגה)

לֹא תִהְיֶה מְשַׁכֵּלָה וַעֲקָרָה בְּאַרְצֶךָ אֶת מִסְפַּר יָמֶיךָ אֲמַלֵּא[א].

הִנֵּה מִקְרָא זֶה הוּא בְּהֶמְשֵׁךְ לְמַה שֶּׁכָּתוּב לִפְנֵי זֶה[ב] וַעֲבַדְתֶּם אֵת הוי׳ אֱלֹקֵיכֶם וּבֵרַךְ אֶת לַחְמְךָ וְאֶת מֵימֶיךָ וַהֲסִירוֹתִי מַחֲלָה מִקִּרְבֶּךָ, וּמַמְשִׁיךְ שֶׁעַל יְדֵי זֶה לֹא תִהְיֶה גַּם כֵּן מְשַׁכֵּלָה וגו׳[ג].

וְהִזְכִּיר כַּאן הַבְטָחָה עַל ג׳ הָעִנְיָנִים דִּבְנֵי חַיֵּי וּמְזוֹנֵי[ד], שֶׁתִּהְיֶה בָּהֶם הַבְּרָכָה בְּרִבּוּי וּבְהַפְלָגָה בְּיוֹתֵר.

וּבֵרַךְ אֶת לַחְמְךָ וְאֶת מֵימֶיךָ הוּא עִנְיַן מְזוֹנֵי, וּמַדְגִּישׁ בַּכָּתוּב וּבֵרַךְ גו׳, הַיְינוּ, שֶׁלֹּא זוֹ בִּלְבָד שֶׁיִּהְיֶה הַמְּזוֹנֵי כְּפִי הַמִּצְטָרֵךְ, אֶלָּא עוֹד זֹאת שֶׁתִּהְיֶה בָּזֶה תּוֹסֶפֶת בְּרָכָה, מְזוֹנָא רְוִיחָא.

וּמַמְשִׁיךְ בַּנּוֹגֵעַ לְחַיֵּי, וַהֲסִירוֹתִי מַחֲלָה מִקִּרְבֶּךָ, וִיתֵירָה מִזֶּה, אֶת מִסְפַּר יָמֶיךָ אֲמַלֵּא, שֶׁהוּא עִנְיַן אֲרִיכוּת יָמִים.

וְכֵן בַּנּוֹגֵעַ לִבְנֵי אוֹמֵר לֹא תִהְיֶה מְשַׁכֵּלָה וַעֲקָרָה, שֶׁזּוֹהִי הַבְּרָכָה דְּלֵדַת בָּנִים (הַשְּׁלִילָה דַּעֲקָרָה) וְהַקִּיּוּם שֶׁלָּהֶם (הַשְּׁלִילָה דִּמְשַׁכֵּלָה), וּבְאֹפֶן שֶׁיִּתְקַיְּמוּ לְאֹרֶךְ יָמִים גַּם לְעֵת זִקְנָתוֹ [כְּפִי שֶׁמָּצִינוּ בְּיַעֲקֹב אָבִינוּ, שֶׁגַּם לְעֵת

---

eases—then there will automatically be no illness, and without illness there are no miscarriages, nobody is barren, and people live a long and healthy life. See *Torat Chaim, Mishpatim* 440a [302c—ed. 2003]; *Or Hatorah, Mishpatim*, p. 1248.

3. *Torat Chaim*, ibid.

cholti], *then I am bereaved.*"[4] [*Shacholti* shares the same root as the Hebrew word for a woman who miscarries, *meshakeilah*]).

INSTRUCTION & ASSURANCE

Regarding these blessings the verse states, *None shall*, which can be interpreted in two ways: 1) as an *instruction* or 2) as an *assurance.*[5] (Examples of the Hebrew wording allowing for the two translations of *instruction* and *assurance* appear in several other instances too.[6]) Thus, the verse can be read as an instruction that *none* shall *miscarry or be barren*, or an assurance that *none* will *miscarry or be barren* as follows: When a person does all that is incumbent upon him not to miscarry or be barren [in his service of G-d, by following the directives that will be explained[7]], then G-d *assures* him that he will indeed not miscarry or be barren [in his service of G-d].

SERVING G-D

The condition for this is, as the verse prefaces, that *You shall serve the L-rd your G-d.* For even though, as our Sages teach regarding the blessing for children, health and livelihood:[8] "It is not dependent upon merit but upon *mazal*"[9]—*mazal* referring to a spiritual level at which no consideration is made for merit—nonetheless, an *abundance* of blessing in children, health and livelihood does depend upon one's service of G-d.[10]

---

4. Genesis 43:14. See *Rashi* on Genesis 27:45.

5. The Hebrew wording of the verse is intentionally open-ended to allow for both translations, since it, in fact, refers to both an instruction and an assurance. The verse therefore is understood to mean that when one carries out the instruction, G-d automatically guarantees the assurance.

6. See *Likkutei Torah, Sukkot* 80d.

7. See below, Ch. 8.

8. *Mo'ed Katan* 28a. See *Or Hatorah, Vayera*, vol. 4, p. 755b ff.; R. Menachem Mendel of Lubavitch, *Biurei Hazohar*, vol. 1, p. 44 ff.; ibid., vol. 2, p. 637 ff.

9. MAZAL (pl. *mazalot*). Lit., "constellations" or "planetary influence." *Mazal* is the root and source of the life-force of vegetation and grass that grows in the physical world. See *True Existence* (Kehot, 2006), p. 32. See, at length, *Overcoming Folly* (Kehot, 2006), pp. 294, 320, 326-356.

During the early development of

זקנתו כאשר חשב שנחסר לו אחד מבניו, אמר ואני כאשר שכלתי שכלתי[ה]].

ובזה אומר לא תהיה גו׳, שיש לפרשו בב׳ אופנים, בלשון צווי ובלשון הבטחה (כפי שמצינו דוגמתו בכמה מקומות[ו]), היינו, צווי שלא תהיה משכלה ועקרה (עס טאר ניט זיין קיין משכלה ועקרה), והבטחה שלא תהיה משכלה ועקרה (עס וועט ניט זיין קיין משכלה ועקרה), היינו, שכאשר האדם עושה התלוי בו שלא תהיה משכלה ועקרה, אזי גם מבטיחו הקדוש ברוך הוא שלא תהיה משכלה ועקרה.

והתנאי לכל זה הוא (כפי שמקדים בכתוב) ועבדתם את הוי׳ אלקיכם, דאף שבנוגע לבני חיי ומזוני אמרו חז״ל[ז] שלאו בזכותא תליא מלתא אלא במזלא תליא מלתא, בחינת המזל שאין ענין הזכות נוגע שם, מכל מקום, רבוי הברכה כו׳ בזה, תלוי בענין העבודה דוקא.

---

civilization, there were people who mistakenly worshipped the constellations. For although *Bereshit Rabbah* (10:6) states, "R. Shimon said: There is not a single herb that does not have a *mazal* in heaven which strikes it and says, 'Grow,'" these people failed to see that their true force is the power of G-d, and that they are only instruments of the divine will, like an ax in the hands of a woodchopper. See *Feminine Faith* (Kehot, 2009), p. 28 ff.

The Talmud (*Mo'ed Katan*, ibid.) states, "Rabbah said: Health, children, and livelihood do not depend upon merit but rather upon *mazal*." Merit cannot change these, because they are pre-determined at the level of the *mazalot*. They form an established part of the fixed conduct of the world, and man cannot tamper with the spiritual influx that is channeled into this world through the *mazalot*. See, however, *Overcoming Folly*, cited above.

10. See *Overcoming Folly*, cited above.

2.

A SERVANT COMPLETES HIS MASTER

[To better comprehend the aforementioned verse] it is necessary to first understand the concept of *avodah*[11] regarding which the verse states *You shall* serve *the L-rd your G-d.*[12]

Seemingly, the entire paradigm of servant and master only applies in this physical world, where a servant can enhance the life of his master [by fulfilling his wishes]. Although a human master is indeed a true master, nevertheless, there are things which he lacks. The function of the servant is to fill the master's needs or to complete his wishes. By doing so, he enhances the life of the master [while the servant himself attains greater realization as well].

Since "G-d is the ultimate of all,"[13] however, it is not readily understood how *avodah*—service—can apply to Him.[14]

DOES G-D CARE?

It is also necessary to resolve an apparent contradiction in the words of our Sages in this regard.[15]

On occasion, we find that the concept of *avodah* does not apply on High. For example, the Midrash states, "For what does the Holy One, blessed be He, care whether a man

---

11. AVODAH. Lit., "service"; in the present context "divine service." In Chabad philosophy, *avodah* also denotes effort, just as physical service requires effort.

The animal soul which descends to the body consists of a mixture of good and evil, with the evil its greater part. Therefore, even when there is an awakening from Above, the animal soul and the body remain unaffected. For although *The spirit of man [the G-dly soul] rises upwards* (Ecclesiastes 3:21), nevertheless, of the animal soul it states, *The spirit of the animal soul descends downwards.* It is specifically man's task to purify the animal soul, and one who does so is called *a server of G-d* (Malachi 3:18). *Avodah* is used in the sense of *orot avudin* ("tanned hides"—עורות עבודין) (*Torah Or, Bereshit* 5b; *Mishpatim* 76a; *Likkutei Torah, Vayikra* 2d; *Transforming the Inner Self* (Kehot, 2004), pp. 44-46).

The root of the word *avodah* comprises the letters *ayin, bet, dalet.* The same root is used to describe the tanning of a hide. By itself, the hide is not suitable for use. It becomes usable leather only after a thorough processing. Likewise, the animal soul becomes fit to serve G-d only through hard work. The person must himself do this work; there is no automatic in-

ב.

וְצָרִיךְ לְהָבִין מַהוּ עִנְיַן הָעֲבוֹדָה, שֶׁעַל זֶה נֶאֱמַר וַעֲבַדְתֶּם אֵת ה׳ אֱלֹקֵיכֶם[ח],

דִּלְכְאוֹרָה, כְּלָלוּת הָעִנְיָן דַּעֲבוֹדַת הָעֶבֶד לַאֲדוֹנוֹ שַׁיָּךְ רַק בְּעֶבֶד וְאָדוֹן לְמַטָּה, שֶׁהָעֶבֶד יָכוֹל לְהוֹסִיף שְׁלֵמוּת אֵצֶל הָאָדוֹן, דְּעִם הֱיוֹתוֹ אָדוֹן, וְאָדוֹן אֲמִתִּי, מִכָּל מָקוֹם, יֵשׁ גַּם עִנְיָנִים שֶׁחֲסֵרִים אֶצְלוֹ, וְזוֹהִי עֲבוֹדַת הָעֶבֶד, לְמַלֹּאת מַחְסוֹרוֹ אוֹ לְהַשְׁלִים אֶת רְצוֹנוֹ, שֶׁעַל יְדֵי זֶה הוּא מַשְׁלִים אֶת הָאָדוֹן [וּמִזֶּה מוּבָן גַּם שֶׁעַל יְדֵי זֶה נַעֲשָׂה תּוֹסֶפֶת שְׁלֵמוּת גַּם אֵצֶל הָעֶבֶד הָעוֹבֵד].

אֲבָל לְמַעְלָה, כֵּיוָן שֶׁאִיהוּ שְׁלִימוּתָא דְכֹלָּא[ט], אֵינוֹ מוּבָן אֵיךְ שַׁיָּךְ שָׁם עִנְיַן הָעֲבוֹדָה[י].

גַּם צָרִיךְ לְהָבִין, שֶׁבְּעִנְיָן זֶה מָצִינוּ סְתִירוֹת בְּדִבְרֵי חַזַ״ל[יא].

דִּלְפְעָמִים מָצִינוּ שֶׁעִנְיַן הָעֲבוֹדָה אֵינוֹ נוֹגֵעַ לְמַעְלָה, כִּדְאִיתָא בְּמִדְרָשׁ[יב] וְכִי אִכְפַּת לֵיהּ לְהַקָּדוֹשׁ

---

spiration as there is for the G-dly soul (*Transforming the Inner Self*, fn. 85).

The term "service" (*avodah*) applies only to what a person does with exertion, contrary to his soul's inclination (*Iggeret Hakodesh*, 12 (*Tanya* 118a-b. Bi-Lingual Edition, pp. 453-455)).

Avodah in the Chasidic lexicon is the act of refinement and improvement of character traits and a development of a deep-rooted inward attachment to G-d (*Hayom Yom*, 6 Tevet).

12. Regarding what follows, see *Maamarei Admur Hazaken 5568*, vol. 1, p. 402; *Or Hatorah*, *Mishpatim*, pp. 1198 ff., 1219 ff. *Sefer Hamaamarim 5662*, p. 273 ff.

13. Introduction to *Tikkunei Zohar* (17b).

14. See discourse entitled *Lo Tihiye Meshakela* in *Torah Or*, *Mishpatim* 78d; *Or Hatorah*, ibid., p. 1255.

15. See *Avodat Hakodesh*, Intro.; ch. 2 (*Chelek Ha'avodah*) and ch. 3, cited in *Shelah*, *Shaar Hagadol*, 29b ff.; *Or Hatorah*, *Mishpatim*, p. 1219 ff.; *Sefer Hamaamarim 5662*, ibid. See also *Sefer Hamaamarim 5678*, p. 282 ff.; *5740*, p. 398 ff.

slaughters an animal from the throat or the nape? The *mitzvot* were given merely for man to be refined."[16] This means that *mitzvot* were given for the sole purpose of refining man and they are of no significance on High. As the verse explicitly states, *If you sinned, what do you do to Him, and if your transgressions are many, what do you do to Him? If you are righteous, what do you give to Him?*[17]

However, at other instances we find that man's service does have influence on High, as the Midrash states[18] regarding the verse, A*nd now, I beseech you, let the power of my L-rd be great*[19]: "When Jews perform the will of G-d, they add strength to the power of Heaven."

Similarly, we find that the lack of *avodah* creates weakness, so to speak, in the heavenly realms. As the Midrash states[20] regarding the verse, *You have weakened the rock that gave birth to you*[21]: "When Israel does not perform the will of G-d (i.e., when they lack in their performance of Torah and *mitzvot*), they weaken, as it were, the great power of Heaven."

3.

THE SINGULAR MASTER

To explain[22]: Chasidus[23] cites *Avodat Hakodesh*[24] that the aforementioned statement of our Sages, "For what does the Holy One, blessed be He, care...," refers to the Singular Master, source of all sources,[25] who is indeed not concerned at all

---

16. *Bereshit Rabbah* 44, beg. *Tanchuma*, *Shemini* 8.

17. Job 35:6-7.

18. *Eichah Rabbah* 1:33; *Shabbat* 89a; cf. *Likkutei Torah*, *Shelach* 39b ff. *Or Hatorah*, *Shelach*, pp. 469 ff., 472, 479. *Or Hatorah*, *Nach*, vol. 1, p. 679.

19. Numbers 14:17.

20. *Eichah Rabbah* ibid.

21. Deuteronomy 32:18.

22. The following chapter provides a Kabbalistic answer to this question. A more Chasidic answer, which is also the focus of this discourse, begins in chapter 5.

בָּרוּךְ הוּא לְמִי שֶׁשּׁוֹחֵט מִן הַצַּוָּאר אוֹ מִי שֶׁשּׁוֹחֵט מִן הָעֹרֶף, לֹא נִתְּנוּ הַמִּצְוֹת אֶלָּא לְצָרֵף בָּהֶן אֶת הַבְּרִיּוֹת, הַיְינוּ, שֶׁכָּל עִנְיַן הַמִּצְוֹת אֵינוֹ אֶלָּא בִּשְׁבִיל לְצָרֵף בָּהֶן אֶת הַבְּרִיּוֹת, אֲבָל אֵין זֶה נוֹגֵעַ לְמַעְלָה. וְכִמְפֹרָשׁ בִּקְרָא[יג] אִם חָטָאתָ מַה תִּפְעָל בּוֹ וְרַבּוּ פְשָׁעֶיךָ מַה תַּעֲשֶׂה לוֹ, אִם צָדַקְתָּ מַה תִּתֶּן לוֹ.

וְלִפְעָמִים מָצִינוּ שֶׁעֲבוֹדַת הָאָדָם יֵשׁ לָהּ הַשְׁפָּעָה לְמַעְלָה, כִּדְאִיתָא בְּמִדְרָשׁ[יד] עַל הַפָּסוּק[טו] וְעַתָּה יִגְדַּל נָא כֹּחַ אַדְ׳, שֶׁעַל יְדֵי קִיּוּם הַתּוֹרָה וּמִצְוֹת נַעֲשֶׂה עִנְיָן דְּהַגְדָּלָה בְּשֵׁם אַדְ׳.

וְכֵן מָצִינוּ שֶׁעַל יְדֵי הֶעְדֵּר הָעֲבוֹדָה נַעֲשָׂה חֲלִישׁוּת כִּבְיָכוֹל לְמַעְלָה, כִּדְאִיתָא בְּמִדְרָשׁ[טז] עַל הַפָּסוּק[יז] צוּר יְלָדְךָ תֶּשִׁי, דִּבְזְמַן שֶׁאֵין יִשְׂרָאֵל עוֹשִׂין רְצוֹנוֹ שֶׁל מָקוֹם (הַיְינוּ הֶעְדֵּר קִיּוּם הַתּוֹרָה וּמִצְוֹת) מַתִּישִׁין כִּבְיָכוֹל כֹּחַ גְּדֻלָּה שֶׁל מַעְלָה.

ג.

אַךְ הָעִנְיָן הוּא[יח], כַּמּוּבָא בַּחֲסִידוּת[יט] מֵעֲבוֹדַת הַקֹּדֶשׁ[כ], דְּמַה שֶּׁאָמְרוּ רַזַ״ל וְכִי מָה אִכְפַּת לוֹ כו׳ הוּא עַל אָדוֹן יָחִיד שֹׁרֶשׁ הַשָּׁרָשִׁים דְּלֵיהּ לֹא אִכְפַּת לֵיהּ כְּלָל,

---

23. *Sefer Hamaamarim 5677*, p. 195 ff.

24. Referenced above, fn. 15.

25. SINGULAR MASTER, SOURCE OF ALL SOURCES. This unusual expression refers to the highest aspects of G-dliness. This expression appears to have been used by *Avodat Hakodesh* to specifically address the effect of divine service upon the Heavenly realms. The term "master" indicates that service is somewhat relevant at this level. Yet the connotation of "singular" is opposite, implying that He is alone and has no need for this service.

Although divine service does not actually affect this level, there is nonetheless a use for it even there, as will be explained in the continuation of [over the performance of *mitzvot*]. However, for the sake of glory,[26] to influence the supernal heads[27] and to unify the beginning of thought with its end,[28] [the performance of *mitzvot*] is an absolute necessity.[29]

This means that at the level of the Singular Master, source of all sources, *avodah* is not at all applicable. Only with vestment in *seder hishtalshelut*,[30] starting with the aspect of *chochmah*,[31] which begins *hishtalshelut* (*chochmah* is called "the beginning"[32]), and even higher, at the level of *keter*,[33] in its

---

the discourse regarding the function of divine service as it relates to G-d's essence. This is why "Singular Master" is the "source of all sources"—a level that is not related to the finite construct of the spiritual worlds, not even as their source. Rather, it is the "source of sources," removed even from the sources as much as the sources are removed from mundane matters. It is the ultimate reason why everything exists, but does not relate to anything that is even remotely finite.

However, if we grant that there is an ultimate purpose for everything, which would include even divine service attached to lower spiritual realms—when the ultimate plan for everything is fulfilled *through* divine service, the outcome would be of concern to even this highest level of G-dliness. Hence, this variation of the term "master" would apply even at the highest levels of G-dliness.

The discourse will clarify the level within G-dliness to which this expression refers.

26. Glory is not an essential state, but rather a state of vestment, similar to clothing that a person wears but is not a part of the person himself (see *Torah Or, Bereshit* 3a). Serving G-d glorifies Him, just a servant glorifies a king by performing his service. However, the service of G-d does not affect G-d directly; it only adds glory to the level of G-dliness that is vested within the spiritual worlds, not to G-d's essence.

27. SUPERNAL HEADS or THREE HEADS: In Kabbalah, "three heads" refer to the spiritual levels of *keter*, *chochmah* and *binah*. *Keter* contains the purest form of G-dliness, the completely abstract idea before it is developed to apply to the spiritual worlds. All worlds emanate from the state of *keter* but exist there as G-dliness that is void of any independent existence. In *chochmah*, the spiritual worlds exist in their purest form, i.e., they merely exist and are without form or shape (see also fn. 31). *Binah* represents a development of the G-dly force as it unravels and takes shape to suit the structure of the created world. (*Daat* is not counted as one of these three. Wherever *keter* appears, *daat* is not mentioned with *chochmah* and *binah*).

28. This is the divine thought through which the world is created. It begins its development in the three heads (see previous note) but only

וְאָמְנָם לְצֹרֶךְ הַכָּבוֹד לְהַשְׁפִּיעַ עַל הָרָאשִׁים הָעֶלְיוֹנִים לְיַחֵד רֹאשׁ הַמַּחֲשָׁבָה בְּסוֹפָהּ כו׳ צֹרֶךְ גָּמוּר הוּא.

וְהַיְינוּ, דִּבְבְחִינַת אָדוֹן יָחִיד שֹׁרֶשׁ כָּל הַשָּׁרָשִׁים אֵין עִנְיַן הָעֲבוֹדָה נוֹגֵעַ כְּלָל, כִּי אִם בְּהִתְלַבְּשׁוּתוֹ בְּסֵדֶר הַהִשְׁתַּלְשְׁלוּת, הָחֵל מִבְּחִינַת הַחָכְמָה שֶׁהִיא רֵאשִׁית הַהִשְׁתַּלְשְׁלוּת (דְּחָכְמָה הִיא רֵאשִׁית[כא]), וְגַם לְמַעְלָה מִזֶּה, בִּבְחִינַת הַכֶּתֶר, הִנֵּה בִּבְחִינָה הַתַּחְתּוֹנָה שֶׁבָּהּ, בְּחִינַת

---

finds actualization in the lowest world (*Asiyah*) in which human beings serve G-d and complete the purpose of creation. The service of G-d therefore accomplishes this purpose of connecting the beginning of thought with its end—i.e., it brings about the culmination of the original thought, uniting the highest form of divine thought with its earthly fulfillment.

29. To explain: Although *avodah* cannot affect certain higher spiritual realms, however, lower levels are not only affected by *avodah*, but at these levels, serving G-d is a necessity. This is because there is something "lacking" that needs to be filled through the service of G-d.

The discourse proceeds to clarify which levels *avodah* affects and which levels are beyond being affected.

30. SEDER HISHTALSHELUT. A Kabbalistic term that refers to the entire order of existence, or "chain of being," which consists of myriad spiritual realms ("worlds") and chambers that gradually progress (or "devolve") into our lowly physical world. (The word *hishtalshelut* is derived from the word *shalshelet*, which literally means "chain," since, in the order of existence, each realm or world is connected to the realm directly "above" and "below" it—much like a chain whose links are interconnected. See *Torah Or*, *Beshalach* 64b; *Likkutei Torah*, *Berachah* 95b.)

31. CHOCHMAH. *Chochmah*, in human terms, refers to the highest level of the thinking process—the initial, unstructured, flash of insight. In the process of creation, it may be loosely defined as a seminal, highly condensed revelation of G-dly light on its highest level of immanence that is the life-force of all of creation. *Chochmah* is the first of the ten *sefirot* (divine attributes) and thus begins the order of descent and development of the worlds in *seder hishtalshelut*.

32. Hence, the verse *Bereshit bara Elokim…* (*In the beginning, when G-d created…*) is translated by *Targum Yerushalmi* as *Bechuchma b'ra*—"With wisdom, G-d created," the *beit* of *Bereshit* being understood in the instrumental sense. See *Zohar* I:31b; *Torat Chaim*, *Bereshit* 1a; *Siddur Im Dach* 305d.

33. KETER. Lit., "crown," *keter* is a Kabbalistic term referring to a spiritual state that transcends all spiritual worlds, as a crown that is higher than

lower part, *arich*,[33] which is the source of emanations, is the concept of *avodah* indeed applicable; but not to *atik*,[33] the innermost aspect of *keter.*

DEFECTIVE KELIM

The explanation[34] [of how *avodah* can affect the higher realms begins from *chochmah*] is that *avodah* is applicable in *seder hishtalshelut* to both *kelim* and *orot.*[35]

The idea of *kelim* is that they conceal the light,[36] allowing the existence of another entity,[37] for when light shines only the source [of the light] is present leaving no room for another entity. By contrast, *kelim* are the concealment of light that allow for the existence of another, to the extent that—after much *hishtalshelut*—creations [that are distinct

---

and encompasses the head. *Keter* is the intermediary or the transitional state between *Or Ein Sof* (G-d's infinite light) and the finite, defined spiritual worlds. As such, *keter* is comprised of two parts:

a) The inner aspect of *keter*, called *atik yomin*, or *atik*, for it is *ne'etak* (from the root עתק)—completely "removed" and separated from creation and the worlds. Attached to *Or Ein Sof*, *atik* is removed from any association with human service of G-d, since it is transcendent and cannot be affected by the worlds at all.

b) The outer aspect of *keter*, called *arich anpin*, associates with the finite structure of the worlds and the ten *sefirot* that inhabit them. *Arich* is thus related to the created worlds that emanate from it, and is therefore affected by the service of G-d in the lower realms.

34. Regarding the following—see *Sefer Hamaamarim 5677*, p. 200 ff; ibid., p. 196 ff.

35. KELIM and OROT. Lit., "vessels" or "instruments" and "lights," creation is a composite of *orot* and *kelim*. Spiritual light is invisible; it becomes perceptible only in conjunction with something that reflects the light—the *keli* or vessel. Thus, lights and vessels are as inseparable as matter and form. In either case, one is inconceivable without the other. Examples: the power of vision is light, the eye is the *keli*; the mind is light, the brain is *keli*; the idea is light, the words conveying it are the *kelim*.

The light and the vessel must be compatible. The vessel must be a fit for the contents; no container could contain anything beyond its capacity. If the glare of the light is too strong for the eye, the eye will be blinded—it will not see anything and simply will not function. A teacher who wishes to convey an idea (light) to a pupil must reduce it to the pupil's mental grasp (*keli*). Otherwise, the student will only become confused.

An analogy: A word consists of two or more letters. When the letters

אֲרִיךְ, שֶׁהִיא שֹׁרֶשׁ הַנֶּאֱצָלִים, נוֹגֵעַ עִנְיַן הָעֲבוֹדָה, מַה שֶּׁאֵין כֵּן בִּבְחִינַת עַתִּיק, פְּנִימִיּוּת הַכֶּתֶר[כב].

וּבֵאוּר הָעִנְיָן[כג], שֶׁבְּסֵדֶר הַהִשְׁתַּלְשְׁלוּת נוֹגֵעַ עִנְיַן הָעֲבוֹדָה הֵן בְּהַכֵּלִים וְהֵן בְּהָאוֹרוֹת.

דְּהִנֵּה, עִנְיַן הַכֵּלִים שֶׁהוּא הֶעְלֵם הָאוֹר הוּא נְתִינַת מָקוֹם לִמְצִיאוּת דְּזוּלַת[כד]. כִּי, כַּאֲשֶׁר הָאוֹר מֵאִיר אֲזַי יֶשְׁנוֹ רַק הַמָּקוֹר, וְאֵין שׁוּם מְצִיאוּת דְּזוּלַת, אֲבָל כֵּלִים שֶׁהֵם הֶעְלֵם הָאוֹר, הֵם נוֹתְנִים מָקוֹם לִמְצִיאוּת דְּזוּלַת, וְעַד שֶׁבְּרִבּוּי הִשְׁתַּלְשְׁלוּת נִתְהַוָּה מֵהֶם בְּחִינַת נִבְרָאִים. וְלִהְיוֹת שֶׁהַכֵּלִים הֵם עִנְיָן שֶׁל זוּלַת, וְסוֹף

---

join in the proper order into a word, they form a vessel for a concept. If you break up the word into separate letters, the concept vanishes.

Both the *orot* and *kelim* serve a united purpose and work together to form creation. The inherent purpose of creation is for mankind to serve G-d. When the service of G-d is performed, it completes the *keli* that allows a particular spiritual revelation (light) to become revealed in the world. Therefore, the lack of serving G-d creates a blemish in the *kelim* that in turn do not allow the light that would otherwise be revealed in that *keli* to shine. The lack of divine service thus affects both the function and purpose of the *kelim* and the *orot*, preventing them from being revealed in this world.

However, levels of G-dliness that transcend *orot* and *kelim* do not need a purpose to be served in order to exist. The existence of that G-dliness is not for something else. Rather, it exists on its own—for itself—and therefore is not affected by the human service of G-d or lack thereof.

36. LIGHT. Light is used as a favorite metaphor in Kabbalah and Chasidut to represent and describe the various manifestations, emanations and forces of G-dliness. It is often used in contradistinction to what is called *atzmut*—the essence of G-d (see fn. 49). Of all physical phenomena, light is that which most closely approximates what is spiritual, exhibiting as it does freedom from the limitations of matter. For example, it is not corporeal; it delights the soul; it enables one to see. It is also analogous to the nature of divine emanations insofar as light is never separated from its source, spreads itself instantaneously, irradiates all physical objects, does not mix and mingle with any other substance, never *per se* changes, is essential to life in general, and is received and absorbed relative to the capacity of the recipient, and the like. See *Mystical Concepts in Chassidism* (Kehot, 1988), chapter 1.

37. See *Sefer HaArachim—Chabad*, vol. 4, *Orot d'sefirot b'yachas l'kelim*.

entities] are actually created from them. Since the idea of *kelim* is the presence of another—and in the end, after much *hishtalshelut*, distinct creations are actually created by way of them—the service of created beings can have influence at the level of *kelim*. This means that when *avodah* is lacking, it causes a defect in the *kelim*.

LIGHT WITHOUT PURPOSE

Furthermore, *avodah* affects even the light, for although the lack of *avodah* actually affects [directly] only the *kelim* and not the light, nevertheless, the defect in the *keli* causes the light to depart from the *keli*. Departure from the *keli* affects the light as well, since the purpose of light is to shine within the *kelim*.[35] Thus, when the light departs from the *keli* it no longer serves its purpose. This is how *avodah* affects the light as well, since the lack of *avodah* causes the light to depart from the *keli*, and as a result, [the light's] purpose is not fulfilled.

Moreover, *avodah* has an effect even on the light that transcends vestment into *kelim*,[38] since even this light is still the source for the light that becomes vested within *kelim*.

SOURCE OF ALL SOURCES

This is why *avodah* affects *arich*. For *arich* is the source of emanations,[39] and, since *avodah* has an effect on the emanations, as mentioned above [that *avodah* has an effect even on the light], *avodah* affects even the source of emanations (i.e., *arich*).

It is only regarding *atik* that our Sages said, "For what

---

38. Since the entire creation of light is for the purpose of becoming manifest in *kelim*, even the purest form of light that in itself is too abstract and undefined to be constricted to *kelim*, was ultimately also created for this purpose. Therefore, even this light is affected by the defect in the *keli*, for the purpose of its creation is to be the *source* of the light that will *become* manifest in *kelim* and as a result of the damaged *keli* (caused by lack of *avodah*), the light's purpose is not fulfilled.

39. *Eitz Chaim*, *Shaar* 42 (*Shaar Derushei Abiya*), ch.1. Cited in *Sefer Hamaamarim 5677*, ibid.

In terms of creation, *arich*, ex-

סוֹף הִנֵּה עַל יְדֵי רִבּוּי הִשְׁתַּלְשְׁלוּת נַעֲשָׂה מֵהֶם בְּחִינַת נִבְרָאִים, לָכֵן בִּבְחִינַת הַכֵּלִים נוֹגֵעַ עִנְיַן עֲבוֹדַת הַנִּבְרָאִים, וְהַיְינוּ שֶׁעַל יְדֵי הֶעְדֵּר הָעֲבוֹדָה נַעֲשֶׂה פְּגַם בְּהַכֵּלִים.

וְלֹא עוֹד אֶלָּא שֶׁגַּם בְּהָאוֹר נוֹגֵעַ עִנְיַן הָעֲבוֹדָה, דְּהִנֵּה, אַף שֶׁהֶעְדֵּר הָעֲבוֹדָה פּוֹגֵם רַק בְּהַכֵּלִים וְלֹא בְּהָאוֹר, מִכָּל מָקוֹם, עַל יְדֵי הַפְּגַם בְּהַכֵּלִים מִסְתַּלֵּק הָאוֹר מֵהַכְּלִי. וְהַסִּלּוּק מֵהַכְּלִי נוֹגֵעַ גַּם בְּהָאוֹר, שֶׁהֲרֵי כַּוָּנַת הָאוֹר הִיא שֶׁיָּאִיר בְּכֵלִים, וְכַאֲשֶׁר הָאוֹר מִסְתַּלֵּק מֵהַכְּלִי, אֲזַי אֵין הָאוֹר מְמַלֵּא אֶת תַּפְקִידוֹ. וְזֶהוּ שֶׁעִנְיַן הָעֲבוֹדָה נוֹגֵעַ גַּם בְּהָאוֹר, כֵּיוָן שֶׁבְּהֶעְדֵּר הָעֲבוֹדָה נַעֲשֶׂה סִלּוּק הָאוֹר שֶׁמִּסְתַּלֵּק מֵהַכְּלִי, וּבְמֵילָא לֹא נִשְׁלֶמֶת הַכַּוָּנָה שֶׁבּוֹ.

וִיתֵרָה מִזֶּה, שֶׁעִנְיַן הָעֲבוֹדָה נוֹגֵעַ גַּם בְּהָאוֹר שֶׁלְּמַעְלָה מֵהִתְלַבְּשׁוּת בְּכֵלִים, שֶׁהֲרֵי גַּם הָאוֹר שֶׁלְּמַעְלָה מֵהִתְלַבְּשׁוּת בְּכֵלִים הֲרֵי הוּא שֹׁרֶשׁ עַל כָּל פָּנִים לְאוֹר הַמִּתְלַבֵּשׁ בְּכֵלִים.

וְזֶהוּ[כב] שֶׁעִנְיַן הָעֲבוֹדָה נוֹגֵעַ בִּבְחִינַת אֲרִיךְ, כִּי, בְּחִינַת אֲרִיךְ הוּא שֹׁרֶשׁ לְנֶאֱצָלִים[כה], וְכֵיוָן שֶׁבַּנֶּאֱצָלִים נוֹגֵעַ עִנְיַן הָעֲבוֹדָה כַּנַ"ל, לָכֵן גַּם בְּשֹׁרֶשׁ הַנֶּאֱצָלִים (בִּבְחִינַת אֲרִיךְ) נוֹגֵעַ עִנְיַן הָעֲבוֹדָה.

וְרַק בִּבְחִינַת עַתִּיק אָמְרוּ רַזַ"ל וְכִי מָה אִכְפַּת לֵיהּ

---

plained above as the outer part of *keter*, is the expression of G-d's will and purpose in emanating the plane of reality that follows beneath it, or in the words of the discourse, "*Arich* is the source of emanations." (The term "emanations" used here for *Atzilut*, the highest of the Four Worlds, is etymologically connected with the word *etzel* (near), i.e., nearest to the Source of creation, the *Ein Sof*, hence still in a state of infinity.) Thus, the outer aspect of *keter* of *Atzilut* is the expression of G-d's will and purpose in emanating *Atzilut*, and the outer aspect of the *keter* of *Beriah* is the expression of G-d's will and purpose in the creation of *Beriah*, and so on.

does the Holy One, blessed be He, care...," since *atik* is the "Singular Master, source of all sources"—pointedly called the Source of all *sources*, not the Source of emanations, for *atik* is beyond being the Source of emanations.

In truth, *atik* is distant even from sources, since the word *atik* is derived from the Hebrew word *vayaatek*[40]—*and he distanced*—indicating that it is distant even from *arich*, being called "the Source of all sources" only figuratively. At this level, *avodah* has no effect, and about this the verse states, *If you sin, what do you do against him? If your transgressions are multiplied, what do you do to him? If you are righteous, what do you give to him?*[41]

4.

However, it is still necessary to understand how the verse, *You shall serve the L-rd your G-d*, refers (not only at levels within *seder hishtalshelut*, where the concept of *avodah* applies, as mentioned earlier, but also) to a level that transcends *hishtalshelut*.[42]

WHO NARRATED THE TORAH?

This will be understood by first analyzing the wording of this verse, which appears to contradict itself from beginning to end.[43] In the beginning, the verse states, *And you shall serve* the L-rd your G-d, *and* He *shall bless...*, in the third person. Later, the verse states, *And* I *will take away*, in the first person, as if G-d were speaking about Himself!

The resolution of this is based on Nachmanides in the introduction to his commentary on the Torah: "Our teacher

---

40. Genesis 12:8. See *Likkutei Torah*, *Emor* 31d; *Sefer Hamaamarim Melukat*, vol. 2, p. 258 ff. [ed. 2002—vol. 2, p. 407].

41. This ends the Kabbalistic answer, that it is only regarding *atik* that our Sages said, "For what does the Holy One, blessed be He, care...," and *If you sin, what do you do against him...*, but *avodah* does affect *arich*, as it does the light that becomes vested within *kelim*, and as such, the service of created beings can have influence at the level of *kelim*.

The discourse continues by ex-

כו׳, כִּי, בְּחִינַת עַתִּיק הוּא אָדוֹן יָחִיד שֹׁרֶשׁ הַשָּׁרָשִׁים, שֹׁרֶשׁ הַשָּׁרָשִׁים דַּיְקָא, וְלֹא שֹׁרֶשׁ הַנֶּאֱצָלִים, כֵּיוָן שֶׁהוּא לְמַעְלָה מִלִּהְיוֹת שֹׁרֶשׁ לְנֶאֱצָלִים.

וּבֶאֱמֶת נִבְדָּל הוּא גַּם מֵהַשָּׁרָשִׁים, שֶׁהֲרֵי עַתִּיק הוּא מִלְּשׁוֹן וַיַּעְתֵּק[כ], וְהַיְינוּ שֶׁהוּא מֻבְדָּל גַּם מִבְּחִינַת אֲרִיךְ, וּמַה שֶּׁנִּקְרָא שֹׁרֶשׁ הַשָּׁרָשִׁים, אֵינוֹ אֶלָּא בְּשֵׁם הַמֻּשְׁאָל בִּלְבַד. וּבִבְחִינָה זוֹ אֵינוֹ נוֹגֵעַ עִנְיַן הָעֲבוֹדָה, וְעַל זֶה נֶאֱמַר אִם חָטָאתָ מַה תִּפְעָל בּוֹ וְרַבּוּ פְשָׁעֶיךָ מַה תַּעֲשֶׂה לּוֹ, אִם צָדַקְתָּ מַה תִּתֶּן לוֹ וגו׳.

ד.

אָמְנָם עֲדַיִן צָרִיךְ לְהָבִין, דַּהֲרֵי מַה שֶּׁכָּתוּב וַעֲבַדְתֶּם אֵת הוי׳ אֱלֹקֵיכֶם וגו׳, קָאֵי (לֹא רַק עַל מַדְרֵגוֹת דְּסֵדֶר הִשְׁתַּלְשְׁלוּת, שֶׁשָּׁם נוֹגֵעַ עִנְיַן הָעֲבוֹדָה כַּנַּ״ל, אֶלָּא גַּם) עַל בְּחִינָה שֶׁלְּמַעְלָה מֵהִשְׁתַּלְשְׁלוּת.

וּבְהֶקְדֵּם הַדִּיּוּק[כו] בִּלְשׁוֹן הַכָּתוּב, שֶׁיֵּשׁ בּוֹ סְתִירָה מֵרֵישָׁא לְסֵיפָא. דְּבַתְּחִלָּה אוֹמֵר וַעֲבַדְתֶּם אֵת הוי׳ אֱלֹקֵיכֶם וּבֵרַךְ גו׳, בִּלְשׁוֹן נִסְתָּר, כִּשְׁלִישִׁי הַמְדַבֵּר, וְאַחַר כָּךְ אוֹמֵר וַהֲסִירוֹתִי גו׳, בִּלְשׁוֹן נוֹכֵחַ, כִּמְדַבֵּר בְּעַד עַצְמוֹ.

וְהָעִנְיָן הוּא[כז], עַל פִּי מַה שֶּׁכָּתַב הָרַמְבַּ״ן בְּהַקְדָּמָתוֹ לְפֵרוּשׁוֹ עַל הַתּוֹרָה, שֶׁלֹּא כָתַב מֹשֶׁה רַבֵּנוּ הַתּוֹרָה (ד׳

---

amining how *avodah* can apply to a level that transcends *hishtalshelut*.

42. As mentioned above, the lack of divine service only affects the *orot* and *keilim*. *Orot* and *kelim* only exist within *seder hishtalshelut*, as beyond *seder hishtalshelut* there are no *orot* and *kelim*, and thus, divine service cannot have an effect there.

43. This analysis appears in *Or Hatorah, Mishpatim* pp. 1219, 1239 and *Sefer Hamaamarim 5662*, p. 272.

Moses did not write the Torah (the first four books[44]) in the first person...but in the third person." The narrator is neither Moses, nor G-d's name *Havaya*,[45] but seemingly a third person, as evident from: *Havaya spoke to Moses saying*. This is not Moses speaking, for in that case, it would have stated "And *Havaya* spoke to *me*," nor are these the words of *Havaya*, for it would have stated "And *I* spoke to Moses." Rather, it is (not *Havaya*, or Moses, but) seemingly a third entity who narrates and tells of the words of *Havaya* to Moses.

THE THIRD ENTITY

The explanation for this is that the "third person" is transcendent: It transcends Moses and even transcends G-d's name, *Havaya*. Although the name *Havaya* represents past, present and future as one,[46] it nonetheless relates to creation[47] (i.e., to *hishtalshelut*).[48] The aspect that transcends both of them (Moses and *Havaya*) is the quintessence of the Infinite,[49] blessed be He. It is He who speaks and tells about the words of *Havaya* to Moses[50] (i.e., relating what transpires within *hishtalshelut*[51]).

[*Atzmut*] is specifically called "third" as is similarly found in the verse, After *two days, he will revive us; on the third day, He will raise us up*.[52] It is known[53] that *after* two *days he will re-*

---

44. The fifth book, Deuteronomy, is primarily a revision, by Moses, of all the events that occurred with the Jewish people following the Exodus. It therefore refers to him in the first person: *and I spoke*; *and I ascended*, and so on.

45. HAVAYA. The Ineffable Divine Name, or Tetragrammaton, composed of the four letters Y-H-V-H, and pronounced in conversation as *Havaya*. There are numerous Hebrew names for G-d in Scripture, each of which expresses a different aspect or attribute of the Divinity. *Havaya* refers to G-d the Infinite, transcending creation and nature, time and space completely—the level of G-dliness which brings everything into existence *ex nihilo*. Thus, although *Havaya* indicates transcendent G-dliness, it nonetheless relates to *seder hishtalshelut* and G-d's involvement in creation, as will be explained.

46. *Zohar* III:257b (*Raaya Mehemnah*); *Pardes*, *Shaar* 1, ch. 9; *Shaar Hayichud v'HaEmunah*, ch. 7.

47. *Pardes*, ibid. *Shaar Hayichud v'HaEmunah*, ch. 4. See *Zohar*, ibid.

48. See *Ateret Rosh*, *Shaar Rosh Hashanah*, ch. 4.

49. ATZMUT UMAHUT EIN SOF, in the Hebrew. Lit., "self and essence," or "es-

סְפָרִים רִאשׁוֹנִים) כִּמְדַבֵּר בְּעַד עַצְמוֹ כו׳ אֶלָּא כִּשְׁלִישִׁי הַמְדַבֵּר, הַיְינוּ, כְּאִלּוּ אֵין הַמְדַבֵּר שֵׁם הוי׳ וְלֹא מֹשֶׁה, אֶלָּא כִּשְׁלִישִׁי הַמְדַבֵּר. וּכְמוֹ וַיְדַבֵּר הוי׳ אֶל מֹשֶׁה לֵּאמֹר, שֶׁאֵין זֶה דִבּוּרוֹ שֶׁל מֹשֶׁה, שֶׁאָז הָיָה צָרִיךְ לוֹמַר וַיְדַבֵּר הוי׳ אֵלַי, וְכֵן אֵין זֶה דִבּוּרוֹ שֶׁל הוי׳, שֶׁאָז הָיָה צָרִיךְ לוֹמַר וָאֲדַבֵּר אֶל מֹשֶׁה, אֶלָּא הוּא כִּשְׁלִישִׁי (לֹא הוי׳ וְלֹא מֹשֶׁה) הַמְדַבֵּר וּמְסַפֵּר אוֹדוֹת דִּבּוּרוֹ שֶׁל הוי׳ אֶל מֹשֶׁה.

וּמְבֹאָר בָּזֶה, דִּשְׁלִישִׁי הַמְדַבֵּר הוּא לְמַעְלָה מִשְּׁנֵיהֶם, לְמַעְלָה מִבְּחִינַת מֹשֶׁה, וּלְמַעְלָה גַּם מִבְּחִינַת שֵׁם הוי׳, כִּי, שֵׁם הוי׳, עִם הֱיוֹתוֹ הָיָה הֹוֶה וְיִהְיֶה כְּאֶחָד[כח], הֲרֵי הוּא שַׁיָּךְ לְהִתְהַוּוּת[כט] (לְהִשְׁתַּלְשְׁלוּת)[ל], וְהַבְּחִינָה שֶׁלְּמַעְלָה מִשְּׁנֵיהֶם (מֹשֶׁה וַהוי׳) הוּא עַצְמוּת וּמַהוּת אֵין סוֹף בָּרוּךְ הוּא, שֶׁהוּא הַמְדַבֵּר וּמְסַפֵּר (עֶר דֶערְצֵיילְט וואָס אִיז פָאָרְגֶעקוּמֶען אִין סֵדֶר הִשְׁתַּלְשְׁלוּת) אוֹדוֹת הַדִּבּוּר דְּשֵׁם הוי׳ אֶל מֹשֶׁה.

וְנִקְרָא שְׁלִישִׁי דַוְקָא, עַל דֶּרֶךְ מַה שֶּׁכָּתוּב[לא] יְחַיֵּנוּ מִיּוֹמָיִם בַּיּוֹם הַשְּׁלִישִׁי וגו׳, כַּיָּדוּעַ[לב] שֶׁיְּחַיֵּנוּ מִיּוֹמָיִם קָאֵי עַל כְּלָלוּת הַהִשְׁתַּלְשְׁלוּת שֶׁנֶּחְלָק לִשְׁתַּיִם, בְּחִינַת

---

sence and substance," the phrase refers to the essence of G-d, or G-d Himself, beyond all definition. Transcending all description, *atzmut* cannot possibly be defined or evaluated in any way, or have any attributed properties.

50. The communication between *Havaya* and Moses that is described in the Torah refers to a degree of divine revelation that was communicated to Moses and that Moses in turn perceived. As most references to G-d in the Torah are in the third person, they refer to a degree of divine revelation, and not directly to G-d's essence. At the Giving of the Torah, however, G-d referred to His essence in first person—"I am the Lord your G-d" (Exodus 20:2).

51. These parenthetical remarks appear in the original transcript, in Yiddish: עֶר דֶערְצֵיילְט וואָס אִיז פָאָרְגֶעקוּמֶען אִין סֵדֶר הִשְׁתַּלְשְׁלוּת.

52. Hosea 6:2. Literally, this verse speaks of the resurrection that will occur after the coming of Moshiach. *Two days* refers to a revelation of *seder hishtalshelut*, which is divided into two, and *the third day* refers to the revelation of the quintessence of the Infinite, as the text proceeds to explain.

53. See *Or Hatorah*, *Mishpatim* p.

vive us refers to the totality of *hishtalshelut*, which is divided into two: *memalei kol almin*, and *sovev kol almin*;[54] *orot* and *kelim*;[55] light as it stands on its own and as it is revealed to another.[56] *On the third day* refers to the revelation of the quintessence of the Infinite, blessed be He.[57]

1219; *Sefer Hamaamarim 5662*, p. 284; *Likkutei Torah, Derushim L'Rosh Hashanah* 64a. See also *Or Hatorah*, ibid., p. 1251; *Torat Chaim, Mishpatim* 438b [301c—ed. 2003].

54. MEMALEI—SOVEV (IMMANENCE—TRANSCENDENCE): *Memalei kol almin* and *sovev kol almin* are two distinct manners by which divine energy is transmitted to creation. *Memalei* refers to the divine energy invested within creation, while *sovev* refers to the divine energy that transcends creation.

Memalei kol almin is immanent divine energy, measured and limited in accordance with that which is being animated. Since it is limited, it permeates all of creation and is interactive with and responsive to the subject that it enlivens. By way of analogy, the life-force from the soul is clothed within the body in a way that alters the body fundamentally. It is not simply a life-force which enlivens any body; it is the life-force of this body, that which transforms it from a dead corpse into a live body.

Sovev kol almin, on the other hand, acts in a remote, imperative, uni-directional manner (i.e., solely from above to below, but not vice versa).

An analogy: Sunlight shines into a room and illuminates it. However, the room itself is not changed thereby, since the light emanates from a source outside of the room; it is not the room itself that lights up. Even when the light illuminates the room, the walls of the room do not actually absorb the light. The light is merely there as light—an illumination from the luminary—but does not become part of that which it illuminates. Similarly, the energy of *sovev* is of an infinite order that cannot be confined within limited creatures. It thus encompasses them in a transcending way. This is why it is called *makif*: it is there, but remains remote from that which it animates. (See *Tanya*, chapters 46 and 48; *Sefer Hamaamarim 5703*, p. 31.)

55. Within the lower realm of *memale*, all of *seder hishtalshelut* (see fn. 30) is comprised of these two components (see fn. 35).

56. LIGHT AS IT STANDS ON ITS OWN and LIGHT AS IT IS REVEALED TO ANOTHER is an even higher division of *seder hishtalshelut* into two distinct categories. The aforementioned distinctions (*memale* and *sovev*, and *orot* and *kelim*) are all within the realm of light that is revealed to another, since they are all forms of outward revelation, for the sake of the existence of the worlds.

The difference between light as it stands on its own and light that is revealed to another can be understood by the analogy of an idea as it is understood by the mind and as it is conveyed to another. Even when a person

מְמַלֵּא כָּל עָלְמִין וּבְחִינַת סוֹבֵב כָּל עָלְמִין, בְּחִינַת אוֹרוֹת וּבְחִינַת כֵּלִים, בְּחִינַת הָאוֹר כְּמוֹ שֶׁהוּא לְעַצְמוֹ וְהַגִּלּוּי כְּמוֹ שֶׁהוּא לְזוּלָתוֹ, וּבַיּוֹם הַשְּׁלִישִׁי קָאֵי עַל עַצְמוּת וּמַהוּת אֵין סוֹף בָּרוּךְ הוּא.

---

thoroughly understands a concept, he must still reorganize it in his mind in order to convey it effectively to a second person. Similarly, light as it stands on its own is infinite, and is not defined and organized like the more limited light that is to be revealed to another.

However, even the light as it stands on its own is a form of divine expression and is not part of G-d's essence. This light is therefore part of the "two" (in the verse) that comprise *hishtalshelut*, as opposed to the "third" aspect that represents the essence of G-d.

57. To explain the quality of three over one: The number one emphasizes that there is only one entity; two denotes division; three unites the previous two. *Chesed*, the first G-dly attribute, indicates the higher extending to the lower; *gevurah*, the second attribute, indicates the lower rising toward the higher, while *tiferet*, the third attribute, harmonizes and unifies both of these elements. *Tiferet* is thus referred to as "truthful" for it contains both opposing preceding characters. In *tiferet*, both *chesed* and *gevurah* are of equal importance, and are synchronized to produce a stable, balanced and fair system for creation. So although in relation to G-dliness, the number one seems to be the highest and most important, true unity is only attainable when aware of another entity, yet we retain the unity. If we are unaware of the other entity, there is no guarantee that the unity is truthful.

Take, for example, the three months of Nissan, Iyar, and Sivan. In the first month, Nissan, G-d liberated the Jewish people from Egypt. This revelation from on High was in a manner that absolutely did not consider the limitations that result from the perspective of the physical world ("the higher to the lower"). In the second month, Iyar, the daily counting of the Omer indicates the step-by-step refinement of character, i.e., interacting with the "other entity," the physical, albeit to transform it ("the lower to the higher"). It is specifically in the *third* month, Sivan, that the Torah was given—for it is specifically when we are aware of this "other entity" that we can express true unity with G-d—in the form of receiving the Torah—true oneness. This also explains the verse in Malachi (2:6), *a Torah of truth*, and the fact that the Torah was given *on the third day* (Exodus 19:16), which indicates the appearance of G-d's essence at the giving of the Torah (*Or Hatorah*, ibid., p. 1219). (*Likkutei Sichot*, vol. 2, pp. 301-302. See *Likkutei Sichot*, vol. 8, p. 105, regarding the giving of the Torah specifically in the *third* millennium after creation; *Likkutei Sichot*, vol. 9, p. 27, regarding the three Holy Temples.)

SERVING HAVAYA AND SERVING ATZMUT

This is why the verse first states, *And you shall serve Havaya your G-d, and He shall bless...*: The Narrator of the Torah says that when *you will serve Havaya your G-d*, then *He shall bless your bread and your water*—that is, *Havaya* (regarding whom it is stated, *And you shall serve Havaya your G-d*) *shall bless your bread and your water.*

Later, the verse states *And I will remove illness from your midst.* The direct language of *And **I** will remove illness* means that the Narrator Himself says that He *will remove illness from your midst.*

From this is understood that the concept of *avodah* applies (not only to the level of G-d's name, *Havaya*, but also) to the Narrator of the Torah, the quintessence of the Infinite, blessed be He. *Avodah* causes (not only that *He shall bless your bread and your water* through the name *Havaya*, but also) *And I will remove illness*—through the quintessence of the Infinite, blessed be He.

This requires further explanation, since, regarding spiritual levels that are higher than *hishtalshelut*, the verse states, *If you are righteous, what do you give to him?*[58] (as mentioned earlier).

5.

It can be said that the teaching of our Sages, "For what does the Holy One, blessed be He, care...," refers to *avodah* itself (i.e., the details of the service). However, the outcome of *avodah*, [which is performed] "in order that creation be refined"—that even a mere creation[59] (and a lowly creation at that) becomes refined and elevated—is in effect the transformation of "something into nothing" and has an impact even on the quintessence of the Infinite.[60]

---

58. Stating that the quintessence of the Infinite, blessed be He, will remove the illness as a result of Israel's *avodah* contradicts the aforementioned concept that *avodah* cannot affect the quintessence of the Infinite.

59. See *Tanya*, ch. 32.

וְזֶהוּ שֶׁבַּתְּחִלָּה נֶאֱמַר וַעֲבַדְתֶּם אֵת הוי' אֱלֹקֵיכֶם וּבֵרַךְ וגו', שֶׁשְּׁלִישִׁי הַמְדַבֵּר אוֹמֵר דְּכַאֲשֶׁר וַעֲבַדְתֶּם אֵת הוי' אֱלֹקֵיכֶם, אֲזַי וּבֵרַךְ אֶת לַחְמְךָ וְאֶת מֵימֶיךָ, הַיְינוּ, שֶׁהוי' (שֶׁעָלָיו נֶאֱמַר וַעֲבַדְתֶּם אֵת הוי' אֱלֹקֵיכֶם) יְבָרֵךְ אֶת לַחְמְךָ וְאֶת מֵימֶיךָ.

וּלְאַחַר זֶה מוֹסִיף וַהֲסִירוֹתִי מַחֲלָה מִקִּרְבֶּךָ, וַהֲסִירוֹתִי לְשׁוֹן נוֹכֵחַ, שֶׁשְּׁלִישִׁי הַמְדַבֵּר אוֹמֵר שֶׁהוּא בְּעַצְמוֹ יָסִיר מַחֲלָה מִקִּרְבֶּךָ.

וּמִזֶּה מוּבָן שֶׁעִנְיַן הָעֲבוֹדָה נוֹגֵעַ (לֹא רַק לְשֵׁם הוי', אֶלָּא) גַּם לִשְׁלִישִׁי הַמְדַבֵּר, בְּחִינַת עַצְמוּת וּמַהוּת אֵין סוֹף בָּרוּךְ הוּא, שֶׁהָעֲבוֹדָה פּוֹעֶלֶת (לֹא רַק וּבֵרַךְ אֶת לַחְמְךָ וְאֶת מֵימֶיךָ עַל יְדֵי שֵׁם הוי', אֶלָּא גַּם) וַהֲסִירוֹתִי מַחֲלָה גו' עַל יְדֵי עַצְמוּת וּמַהוּת אֵין סוֹף בָּרוּךְ הוּא.

וְצָרִיךְ לְהָבִין, הֲרֵי בִּבְחִינָה שֶׁלְּמַעְלָה מֵהִשְׁתַּלְשְׁלוּת כְּתִיב[יג] אִם צָדַקְתָּ מַה תִּתֶּן לוֹ (כַּנַּ"ל).

ה.

וְיֵשׁ לוֹמַר, שֶׁזֶּה שֶׁאָמְרוּ רַזַ"ל וְכִי מָה אִכְפַּת לֵיהּ לְהַקָּדוֹשׁ בָּרוּךְ הוּא כו', קָאֵי עַל הָעֲבוֹדָה עַצְמָהּ (דְּהַיְינוּ פְּרָטֵי הָעֲבוֹדָה), אֲבָל הַתּוֹצָאָה שֶׁל הָעֲבוֹדָה שֶׁעַל יָדָהּ נַעֲשֶׂה צֵרוּף הַבְּרִיּוֹת, שֶׁגַּם בִּבְרִיּוֹת בְּעָלְמָא[לג] בְּרִיָּה פְּחוּתָה, נַעֲשֶׂה צֵרוּף וְזִכּוּךְ, שֶׁזֶּהוּ עִנְיַן הָאִתְהַפְּכָא מִיֵּשׁ לְאַיִן, הִנֵּה זֶה נוֹגֵעַ גַּם בִּבְחִינַת הָעַצְמוּת[לד].

---

60. See *B'shaah Shehikdimu, 5712*, where it is explained how, although the service of G-d itself does not affect *atzmut*, the outcome of serving G-d, i.e., the refining of creation, is the fulfillment of G-d's desire that is rooted in *atzmut*.

Tanchuma, *Nasso* 16:16 (Warsaw

It is regarding this that the verse states, *And you shall serve Havaya your G-d...and* I *will take [illness] away...*, referring specifically to the quintessence of the Infinite, blessed be He.[61]

REMOVING ILLNESS

This explains why the verse *And I will remove illness from your midst* is different from an earlier verse, *I will put none of the diseases which I have brought upon the Egyptians upon you.*[62] The verse *and I will put none of the diseases* connotes the possibility for disease and the blessing is that this possibility will not be actualized. However, in the verse *And I will remove illness*, there is a greater novelty, in that even when there is actual disease (not just the potential for disease) the disease will be removed. In order to remove a disease that already actually exists there is a need for an even greater force. This is the meaning of the verse *And* I *will take away*, speaking directly to the second person, since this refers to the quintessence of the Infinite, blessed be He.[63]

6.

KABBALAT OL

The concept of *avodah* [mentioned in the verse] *And you shall serve the L-rd your G-d* is like the service of a servant. It primarily refers to serving with awe and *kabbalat ol*, acceptance of the yoke of Heaven, that comprises the labor of a servant.[64]

A servant shows no consideration for himself and is not

---

ed.), states: "When the Holy One, blessed be He, created the world, He desired that He have a dwelling place in the lower realms." (See *Tanya*, ch. 36, for an explanation of this desire.)

Chasidus explains that this desire of G-d is rooted in *atzmut* and Rabbi Schneur Zalman of Liadi said of this Midrash: "Concerning a desire there can be no questions." G-d's desire is beyond question since it is rooted in His essence. See *Or Hatorah, Balak*, p. 997; *Yom Tov Shel Rosh Hashanah 5666*, p. 7.

In the infinitude of *atzmut*, even two opposites can be true. G-d can desire without lacking—i.e., the desire remains a true desire, yet He truly lacks nothing. Similarly, *atzmut* desires the outcome of the service of G-d (the refining of creation), yet He does not lack anything so that He

וְעַל זֶה נֶאֱמַר וַעֲבַדְתֶּם אֵת הוי׳ אֱלֹקֵיכֶם גו׳ וַהֲסִירוֹתִי גו׳, עַצְמוּת וּמַהוּת אֵין סוֹף בָּרוּךְ הוּא דַּוְקָא.

וּבָזֶה יוּבַן מַה שֶּׁנֶּאֱמַר כַּאן וַהֲסִירוֹתִי מַחֲלָה מִקִּרְבֶּךָ, וְלֹא כְּמוֹ שֶׁנֶּאֱמַר לִפְנֵי זֶה[סב] כָּל הַמַּחֲלָה אֲשֶׁר שַׂמְתִּי בְמִצְרַיִם לֹא אָשִׂים עָלֶיךָ גו׳, כִּי, בַּפָּסוּק כָּל הַמַּחֲלָה גו׳ לֹא אָשִׂים גו׳, מְדֻבָּר רַק אוֹדוֹת אֶפְשָׁרוּת לְמַחֲלָה, וְהַבְּרָכָה הִיא שֶׁאֶפְשָׁרוּת זוֹ לֹא תָבוֹא לְפֹעַל. אֲבָל בַּפָּסוּק וַהֲסִירוֹתִי מַחֲלָה גו׳ יֵשׁ חִדּוּשׁ גָּדוֹל יוֹתֵר, שֶׁגַּם כְּשֶׁיֶּשְׁנָהּ מַחֲלָה בְּפֹעַל (לֹא רַק אֶפְשָׁרוּת לְמַחֲלָה), תִּהְיֶה הֲסָרַת הַמַּחֲלָה. וּבִשְׁבִיל הֲסָרַת הַמַּחֲלָה שֶׁכְּבָר יֶשְׁנָהּ בְּפֹעַל יֵשׁ צֹרֶךְ בְּכֹחַ עֶלְיוֹן יוֹתֵר, וְעַל זֶה נֶאֱמַר וַהֲסִירוֹתִי בִּלְשׁוֹן נוֹכֵחַ, שֶׁקָּאֵי עַל עַצְמוּת וּמַהוּת אֵין סוֹף בָּרוּךְ הוּא[סג].

ו.

וְהִנֵּה עִנְיַן הָעֲבוֹדָה, וַעֲבַדְתֶּם אֵת הוי׳ אֱלֹקֵיכֶם, שֶׁהִיא בְּדֻגְמַת עֲבוֹדַת הָעֶבֶד, קָאֵי בְּעִקָּר עַל הָעֲבוֹדָה בְּיִרְאָה וְקַבָּלַת עֹל[סד], שֶׁהִיא עֲבוֹדַת עֶבֶד[סה],

שֶׁהָעֶבֶד אֵינוֹ תּוֹפֵס מָקוֹם לְעַצְמוֹ, וְעוֹד יוֹתֵר

---

might need the service itself for His completion or for Him to be called a master because of it. verse therefore assures that when you serve *Havaya*, then *atzmut* (not *Havaya*) will remove the illness from you.

61. Although the actual service of G-d is the service of *Havaya* and does not have an impact on *atzmut*, the *outcome* of serving G-d (the fact that a mere creation has been refined and elevated through the service of G-d) has an impact in some way even on *atzmut*. The

62. Exodus 15:26.

63. See Ch. 7.

64. *Tanya* ch. 41; *Kuntres Ha'avodah*, ch. 2. See *Likkutei Sichot*, vol. 7, p. 183.

an entity of his own;[65] he is completely nullified to the [will of the] master. Although he would prefer to be free,[66] he nevertheless constricts and selflessly devotes himself to the master,[67] and therefore performs and fulfills all of his master's wishes.

This is why the first and primary service [of G-d], the foundation of all *avodah*, is the service of *kabbalat ol*.[64] Even when one has not yet transformed his natural self and retains his own wishes, perspectives, and feelings [not having developed an appreciation for the Master's wishes], he nevertheless labors in his work with *kabbalat ol*. Since when it comes to deed (performing *mitzvot* by refraining from involvement in evil and by doing good deeds[68]) a person cannot wait until he changes his essence, then even while still in his current state, he must go about his service of G-d with *kabbalat ol*.[69]

This is likewise the order of the routine daily service. The service of the day begins with the recitation of *Modeh ani* ["I offer thanks"],[70] and the service of [the morning] prayer begins with *Hodu LaHashem* ["Offer praise to the L-rd"]. Thus, before the appropriate contemplation while reciting the Verses of Praise and before the contemplation while reciting the Blessings of the *Shema* and the actual recitation of the *Shema* and the Amidah—we recite *Hodu LaHashem*, an acknowledgement that reflects a service of G-d in a manner of *kabbalat ol*.[71]

---

65. See *Kiddushin* 23b and *Rashba*, there, that a servant is not an independent entity that can receive gifts or own possessions.

66. See *Gittin* 13a. See also *Sefer Hamaamarim Melukat*, vol. 1, p. 308 ff. [ed. 2002—vol. 3, p. 10].

67. See *Kuntres Ha'avodah*, ibid.

68. See Psalms 34:15 and 37:27, *Depart from evil, and do good.*

69. The person must not wait until he has transformed himself into a proper servant of G-d before starting to fulfill G-d's commandments with

שֶׁאֵינוֹ שׁוּם מְצִיאוּת לְעַצְמוֹ[לט], וְהוּא בְּבִטּוּל אֶל הָאָדוֹן, דְּאַף שֶׁמִּצַּד עַצְמוֹ בְּהֶפְקֵירָא נִיחָא לֵיהּ[מ], הֲרֵי הוּא בְּכִוּוּץ וּבִטּוּל אֶל הָאָדוֹן[מא], וְלָכֵן עוֹשֶׂה וּמְקַיֵּם אֶת רְצוֹנוֹ.

וְזֶהוּ שֶׁרֵאשִׁית הָעֲבוֹדָה וְעִקָּרָהּ וְשָׁרְשָׁהּ הִיא הָעֲבוֹדָה דְּקַבָּלַת עֹל, וְהַיְינוּ, שֶׁלַּמְרוֹת הֱיוֹתוֹ בְּמַעֲמָד וּמַצָּב שֶׁלֹּא שִׁנָּה אֶת עַצְמוֹ, רְצוֹנוֹ, שִׂכְלוֹ וּמִדּוֹתָיו (עֶר הָאט זִיךְ נִיט אִיבֶּערְגֶעמַאכְט אוּן שְׁטֵייט אִין זַיְינֶע רְצוֹנוֹת וכו'), הֲרֵי הוּא עוֹבֵד אֶת עֲבוֹדָתוֹ בְּדֶרֶךְ קַבָּלַת עֹל, שֶׁהֲרֵי בְּהַנּוֹגֵעַ לְמַעֲשֶׂה בְּפֹעַל, קִיּוּם הַמִּצְוֹת בְּסוּר מֵרָע וַעֲשֵׂה טוֹב, אִי אֶפְשָׁר לְהַמְתִּין עַד שֶׁיְּשַׁנֶּה אֶת עַצְמוֹ, אֶלָּא גַּם בִּהְיוֹתוֹ בְּמַעֲמָדוֹ וּבְמַצָּבוֹ כְּמוֹ שֶׁהוּא, צָרִיךְ לַעֲבוֹד עֲבוֹדָתוֹ בְּקַבָּלַת עֹל.

וְכֵן הוּא בְּסֵדֶר הָעֲבוֹדָה בְּכָל יוֹם וָיוֹם, שֶׁהַתְחָלַת עֲבוֹדַת הַיּוֹם הִיא בַּאֲמִירַת מוֹדֶה אֲנִי[מב], וְכֵן בַּעֲבוֹדַת הַתְּפִלָּה, הַהַתְחָלָה הִיא הוֹדוּ לַהוי', שֶׁעוֹד לִפְנֵי הַהִתְבּוֹנְנוּת דִּפְסוּקֵי דְזִמְרָה, וְלִפְנֵי הַהִתְבּוֹנְנוּת דְּבִרְכוֹת קְרִיאַת שְׁמַע, קְרִיאַת שְׁמַע וּשְׁמוֹנֶה עֶשְׂרֵה, אוֹמֵר הוּא הוֹדוּ לַהוי', בְּחִינַת הוֹדָאָה, שֶׁזּוֹהִי הָעֲבוֹדָה בְּדֶרֶךְ קַבָּלַת עֹל דַּוְקָא.

---

kabbalat ol, since he is from the start required to fulfill the commandments actively and to refrain from violating the prohibitions. This is only with respect to deed, however; intent and devotion are an entirely different matter. They are processes that can be worked on and improved over time.

70. See *Kuntres Ha'avodah*, ch. 1.

71. The Hebrew words "*modeh*" and "*hodu*" come from the Hebrew root *hoda'ah* ("submission"). These are statements of *kabbalat ol*, submission to the yoke of the higher power. See also *The Path to Selflessness* (Kehot, 2009), p. 17 and pp. 26-28.

7.

LOVE & PRAYER

However, [the service of G-d is not limited to *kabbalat ol* alone,] since the verse *And you shall* serve *the L-rd your G-d* refers to the service of prayer (as well), [which involves developing a love for G-d]. As Maimonides writes:[72] "It is a positive mitzvah to pray...as the verse states: *And you shall serve the L-rd your G-d.* From tradition we know that this refers to the service of prayer, as the verse states:[73] *And to serve him with all your heart.* Regarding this our Sages have said,[74] 'What is the service of the heart? It is prayer.'" It is implicit that this includes (in addition to serving G-d out of awe) also serving Him with love. This is the concept of prayer regarding which the *Zohar* states, "There is no worship of G-d that can be compared to the worship of love."[75]

The reason why prayer must involve serving G-d with love is because[76] prayer affects both the G-dly soul and the animal soul.[77] The Hebrew word for prayer, *tefillah*, is related to the word *tofel*,[78] to connect, since through prayer the G-dly soul is connected with its spiritual source.

An additional effect of prayer is that it refines the animal soul[79] and elevates the spiritual sparks[80] within the body and its portion of the world.[81]

---

72. Laws of Prayer, beg.

73. Deuteronomy 11:13.

74. *Taanit* 2a.

75. See *Zohar* II:55b; III:267a. See also *Likkutei Torah*, *Shelach* 42c; *Kuntres Ha'avodah*, ch.1; ch. 3 ff. *Sefer HaArachim—Chabad*, vol. 1, *Ahavat Hashem*, 5; ibid., 9.

76. Regarding the following, see *Kuntres Ha'avodah*, chs. 1-3.

77. G-DLY SOUL and ANIMAL SOUL. *Tanya* (chs. 1, 2, 9, and 12) speaks of man having two states of consciousness, which derive from the G-dly soul and the animal soul. The animal soul stems from *kelipat nogah* and seeks only self-gratification. The G-dly soul, which is "literally a part of G-d" (*Tanya*, ch. 2), seeks to cleave to G-d through constant awareness of Him and fulfillment of His will.

The two souls struggle for dominion over the body and it is man's task to grant authority to the G-dly soul, and to have the G-dly soul transform the animal soul and harness its energy for holiness. See *Tanya*, chapters 1, 2, 9, and 12.

ז.

אָמְנָם כֵּיוָן שֶׁהַפָּסוּק וַעֲבַדְתֶּם אֵת הוי' אֱלֹקֵיכֶם קָאֵי (גַּם) עַל עִנְיַן הַתְּפִלָּה, כְּמוֹ שֶׁכָּתַב הָרַמְבַּ"ם[מג] מִצְוַת עֲשֵׂה לְהִתְפַּלֵּל כו' שֶׁנֶּאֱמַר וַעֲבַדְתֶּם אֵת הוי' אֱלֹקֵיכֶם, מִפִּי הַשְּׁמוּעָה לָמְדְנוּ שֶׁעֲבוֹדָה זוֹ הִיא תְּפִלָּה, שֶׁנֶּאֱמַר[מד] וּלְעָבְדוֹ בְּכָל לְבַבְכֶם, אָמְרוּ חֲכָמִים[מה] אֵי זוֹ הִיא עֲבוֹדָה שֶׁבְּלֵב זוֹ תְּפִלָּה, מוּבָן, שֶׁבָּזֶה נִכְלָל (נוֹסָף עַל הָעֲבוֹדָה מִיִּרְאָה) גַּם עִנְיַן הָעֲבוֹדָה מֵאַהֲבָה, שֶׁזֶּהוּ עִנְיַן הַתְּפִלָּה, לֵית פּוּלְחָנָא כְּפוּלְחָנָא דִּרְחִימוּתָא[מו].

וְהָעִנְיָן בָּזֶה, דְּהִנֵּה[מז] פְּעֻלַּת הַתְּפִלָּה הִיא הֵן בְּנֶפֶשׁ הָאֱלֹקִית וְהֵן בְּנֶפֶשׁ הַבַּהֲמִית. כִּי, תְּפִלָּה הוּא מִלְּשׁוֹן תּוֹפֵל[מח], שֶׁהוּא עִנְיַן הַחִבּוּר, שֶׁעַל יָדָהּ נַעֲשֵׂית הִתְחַבְּרוּת נֶפֶשׁ הָאֱלֹקִית עִם שָׁרְשָׁהּ וּמְקוֹרָהּ.

וְעוֹד עִנְיָן בִּתְפִלָּה, שֶׁעַל יָדָהּ נַעֲשֶׂה בֵּרוּר וְזִכּוּךְ נֶפֶשׁ הַבַּהֲמִית, וְהַעֲלָאַת הַנִּיצוֹצוֹת דְּגוּפוֹ וְחֶלְקוֹ בָּעוֹלָם.

---

78. *Kuntres Ha'avodah*, ibid.; *Torah Or*, *Terumah* 79d (see fn. to *Sefer Hamaamarim 5709*, p. 79); see *Torah Or*, *Mishpatim* 79b. *Torat Chaim*, ibid., 434b [298c ff.—ed. 2003]; *Maamarei Admur Hazaken 5568*, p. 402; *Or Hatorah*, *Mishpatim*, p. 1198.

79. By meditating in prayer about the G-dly source of everything earthly, the animal soul's earthly passion can be directed into a passionate love for G-d.

80. NITZOTZOT (sing. NITZOTZ), in the Hebrew. The *Arizal* (*Eitz Chaim*, 39:2) writes that within all physical matter there are *nitzotzot*, sparks of holiness. These sparks comprise the spiritual energy that creates, sustains, and enlivens everything physical. In their natural state, physical matter conceals the sparks. When a Jew serves G-d through Torah study and the performance of *mitzvot* and ensures that "all his deeds are performed for the sake of heaven" (*Avot* 2:12), these sparks become refined and elevated, and return to their source in holiness.

81. That is, that portion of the world which the soul is charged with refining and whose spiritual sparks it must elevate.

In addition to inspiring the animal

These two effects of prayer[82] are achieved specifically by serving G-d out of love, since when one serves G-d out of awe and *kabbalat ol* alone, he does not effect change within himself and does not refine the animal soul.[83]

TRANSFORMATIVE LOVE

It is clearly evident that there are people who are born with a natural awe of Heaven and, with just a little contemplation, are capable of stimulating awe within themselves to resist evil and do good deeds. Nevertheless, even when their conduct in resisting evil and performing good deeds is perfect, their animal soul remains in its original power and strength, and even becomes stronger with the passage of time through frequent use.[84]

Furthermore, because serving G-d out of awe [alone] does not refine the animal soul, it also does not connect the G-dly soul to its spiritual source. The way to connect the G-dly soul to its spiritual source is by fulfilling the will of G-d, and the will of G-d is that the G-dly soul should refine both the body and the animal soul. In order to accomplish this, the soul descended to the world below; since the soul itself is not in need of *tikkun*, repair, it descends to the physical world only to refine the body and animal soul.[85]

Therefore, as long as the person has not refined his animal

---

soul to develop a love for G-d, meditating in prayer about the G-dly source of everything earthly reveals each thing's G-dly nature and purpose, thus redeeming the spiritual sparks of G-dliness that lie hidden within them.

82. Namely: a) the adjoining of the G-dly soul with its spiritual source; b) the refinement of the animal soul, and the elevation of the spiritual sparks of the body and its portion of the world.

83. Awe is capable of suppressing the earthly desires of the animal soul, but not of transforming it or drawing it nearer to G-dliness. Love, however, creates a positive sense of connection that bonds the G-dly soul with its G-dly source and can even envelop the animal soul, igniting within it a passionate love to unite with G-d and to turn itself over to holiness.

84. See *Tanya*, ch. 13. The fact that the animal soul remains un-

וּבְ׳ עִנְיָנִים אֵלּוּ הֵם בְּהָעֲבוֹדָה דְּאַהֲבָה דַּוְקָא. דְּהִנֵּה, בַּעֲבוֹדָה דְּיִרְאָה וְקַבָּלַת עֹל לְבַדָּהּ, הֲרֵי לֹא שִׁנָּה אֶת עַצְמוֹ, וְלֹא פָּעַל בֵּרוּר וְזִכּוּךְ נֶפֶשׁ הַבַּהֲמִית,

וּכְפִי שֶׁרוֹאִים בְּמוּחָשׁ, שֶׁיֶּשְׁנָם כָּאֵלֶּה שֶׁיֵּשׁ לָהֶם יִרְאַת שָׁמַיִם טִבְעִית, וּבְהִתְבּוֹנְנוּת קַלָּה יְכוֹלִים הֵם לְעוֹרֵר אֶת הַיִּרְאָה לִהְיוֹת סוּר מֵרָע וַעֲשֵׂה טוֹב, וְאַף עַל פִּי כֵן, גַּם כַּאֲשֶׁר הַנְהָגָתָם בְּסוּר מֵרָע וַעֲשֵׂה טוֹב הִיא בִּשְׁלֵמוּת, נִשְׁאֶרֶת נַפְשָׁם הַבַּהֲמִית בְּתָקְפָּהּ וּבִגְבוּרָתָהּ כְּתוֹלַדְתָּהּ, וְאַדְרַבָּה, נִתְחַזְּקָה יוֹתֵר בְּהֶמְשֵׁךְ הַזְּמַן עַל יְדֵי רִבּוּי הַהִשְׁתַּמְּשׁוּת בָּהּ[מט].

וְכֵיוָן שֶׁעַל יְדֵי הָעֲבוֹדָה מִיִּרְאָה לֹא פָּעַל בֵּרוּר וְזִכּוּךְ נֶפֶשׁ הַבַּהֲמִית, לֹא פָּעַל גַּם הִתְחַבְּרוּת הַנֶּפֶשׁ הָאֱלֹקִית עִם שָׁרְשָׁהּ וּמְקוֹרָהּ, כִּי, הִתְחַבְּרוּת נֶפֶשׁ הָאֱלֹקִית הִיא עַל יְדֵי מִלּוּי רְצוֹנוֹ יִתְבָּרֵךְ, וַהֲרֵי רְצוֹנוֹ יִתְבָּרֵךְ הוּא שֶׁהַנְּשָׁמָה תְּבָרֵר אֶת הַגּוּף וְנֶפֶשׁ הַבַּהֲמִית, וּבִשְׁבִיל זֶה יָרְדָה הַנְּשָׁמָה לְמַטָּה, שֶׁהֲרֵי הַנְּשָׁמָה עַצְמָהּ אֵינָהּ צְרִיכָה תִּקּוּן, וִירִידָתָהּ לְמַטָּה הִיא כְּדֵי לְבָרֵר אֶת הַגּוּף וְנֶפֶשׁ הַבַּהֲמִית[נ],

וְכָל זְמַן שֶׁלֹּא פָּעַל בֵּרוּר נֶפֶשׁ הַבַּהֲמִית, לֹא מִלֵּא

---

transformed is evident when such a person sins inadvertently. When he is consciously in control of his actions, his awe of G-d keeps him from transgression. However, he can be caught off-guard and transgress inadvertently when he is not actively controlling his actions. This indicates that his animal soul is still strong within him and when left unguarded will attempt to transgress the will of G-d. The animal soul is only transformed by developing a love for G-d, not by awe alone.

Therefore, even when one can find no fault in the person's deeds, it does not mean that he is free of evil. He may possess a powerful animal soul that is unchanged despite all of his successful efforts to resist it. Only by way of love can one direct and transform the powerful animalistic nature of the animal soul and convert it to use it in the service of G-d.

85. See *Tanya*, ch. 37 (48b), from *Eitz Chaim*, *Shaar* 26, ch. 1.

soul, he has not fulfilled the will of G-d, and consequently his G-dly soul does not connect to its spiritual source. Only when he serves G-d out of love—and thereby refines his animal soul—does he actually connect his G-dly soul with its spiritual source.

TOUGH LOVE

Another point to explain why serving G-d out of awe alone does not suffice, and why one must also serve G-d out of love, is as follows:

The word *avodah* is related to the word *ibud*, as in *ibud orot* (tanning hides).[86] Just as tanning calls for a number of activities that require intense exertion until the hide becomes suitable parchment for writing, so must one's service of G-d involve labor and the exertion of tremendous effort.

From this it is understood that serving G-d out of awe is not the ultimate form of service, since serving G-d out of awe does not necessarily involve labor and the exertion of effort, [for,] as mentioned previously, some people possess a natural fear of Heaven. Therefore, one must also serve G-d out of love, since serving G-d out of love can only be a result of labor and effort.[87]

LOVE & AWE

It is now understood that the verse *And you shall serve the L-rd your G-d* refers both to the service of G-d with awe—which is the beginning of G-dly service—and to the service of G-d with love. So it is explained in *Kuntres Ha'avodah*[88]—that the ultimate service of G-d incorporates both awe and love.

---

86. See above, fn. 11.

87. Although there are those who do not possess a natural fear of Heaven and would need to exert effort for divine service out of awe, the labor that

אֶת רְצוֹנוֹ יִתְבָּרֵךְ, וְלָכֵן לֹא פָּעַל הִתְחַבְּרוּת דְּנַפְשׁוֹ הָאֱלֹקִית עִם שָׁרְשָׁהּ וּמְקוֹרָהּ. וְדַוְקָא בַּעֲבוֹדָה מֵאַהֲבָה, שֶׁעַל יָדָהּ פּוֹעֵל בֵּרוּר וְזִכּוּךְ נֶפֶשׁ הַבַּהֲמִית, הֲרֵי הוּא פּוֹעֵל גַּם הִתְחַבְּרוּת נֶפֶשׁ הָאֱלֹקִית עִם שָׁרְשָׁהּ וּמְקוֹרָהּ.

וְעוֹד עִנְיָן בָּזֶה שֶׁלֹּא מַסְפִּיק הָעֲבוֹדָה מִיִּרְאָה אֶלָּא מֻכְרַחַת לִהְיוֹת גַּם הָעֲבוֹדָה מֵאַהֲבָה,

דְּהִנֵּה עֲבוֹדָה הִיא מִלְּשׁוֹן עִבּוּד עוֹרוֹת[נא], וּכְשֵׁם שֶׁבְּעִבּוּד עוֹרוֹת יֵשׁ צֹרֶךְ בְּכַמָּה וְכַמָּה פְּעֻלּוֹת הַבָּאוֹת עַל יְדֵי טִרְחָא וִיגִיעָה גְּדוֹלָה עַד שֶׁנַּעֲשֶׂה הָעוֹר מְעֻבָּד וְרָאוּי לִהְיוֹת קְלָף שֶׁיִּכְתְּבוּ עָלָיו פָּרָשִׁיּוֹת כו׳, כְּמוֹ כֵן צְרִיכָה לִהְיוֹת עֲבוֹדַת ה׳ בְּאֹפֶן שֶׁל עֲבוֹדָה דַּוְקָא, טִרְחָא וִיגִיעָה גְּדוֹלָה.

וּמִזֶּה מוּבָן שֶׁהָעֲבוֹדָה מִיִּרְאָה אֵינָהּ אֲמִתִּית עִנְיַן הָעֲבוֹדָה, כִּי, בְּיִרְאָה אֵין הֶכְרֵחַ שֶׁתִּהְיֶה עֲבוֹדָה וִיגִיעָה גְּדוֹלָה, וְכַנַּ"ל שֶׁיֶּשְׁנָם כָּאֵלֶּה שֶׁיֵּשׁ לָהֶם יִרְאַת שָׁמַיִם טִבְעִית כו׳, וְלָכֵן בְּהֶכְרֵחַ לִהְיוֹת גַּם הָעֲבוֹדָה מֵאַהֲבָה, שֶׁבָּאָה עַל יְדֵי עֲבוֹדָה וִיגִיעָה גְּדוֹלָה דַּוְקָא.

וּמִזֶּה מוּבָן שֶׁמַּה שֶּׁכָּתוּב וַעֲבַדְתֶּם אֵת הוי׳ אֱלֹקֵיכֶם, קָאֵי הֵן עַל הָעֲבוֹדָה מִיִּרְאָה, שֶׁהִיא רֵאשִׁית הָעֲבוֹדָה, וְהֵן עַל הָעֲבוֹדָה מֵאַהֲבָה, וְכִמְבֹאָר בְּקוּנְטְרֵס הָעֲבוֹדָה[נב] שֶׁשְּׁלֵמוּת הָעֲבוֹדָה הִיא הֵן מִיִּרְאָה וְהֵן מֵאַהֲבָה.

---

applies to serving G-d out of love is equal for all.

88. Chs. 1-3.

8.

SPIRITUAL CHILDREN

To clarify the type of service that is alluded to in the verse *And you shall serve the L-rd your G-d*, the verse continues: *None shall miscarry nor be barren.*

The definition of "barren"[89] is that one lacks the ability to bear children, "children" being the characteristics of love and awe (which are born of contemplation[90]). In this analogy, love is characterized as a son and awe as a daughter.[91]

"Miscarriage" means that one gives birth to children but they have no continuity.

The verse thus instructs, *None shall miscarry or be barren*—that contemplation should be practiced in such a manner that it gives birth to emotions, and that the emotions should have continuity; since only then will the requirement of *You shall serve the L-rd your G-d* be suitably fulfilled.

UNINSPIRED

To further clarify this concept:[92]

There are two types of barren women. The first does not even possess a womb,[93] i.e., she lacks the means for becoming pregnant in order to give birth. In the service of G-d, "womb" refers to "intellectual excitement," from which emotions are born and are revealed within the heart.[94] A "barren woman

---

89. Regarding the following—see *Torah Or, Mishpatim* 79a ff.; *Torat Chaim*, ibid., 431b [296d—ed. 2003] ff.; *Or Hatorah*, ibid., p. 1256 ff.; *Sefer Hamaamarim 5692*, p. 222.

90. See *Tanya*, ch. 3.

91. Although both men and women are equally capable of developing both a love and awe of G-d, characteristically, love is a more masculine trait. This is alluded to in the homiletic interpretation of the verse (Psalms 98:3) *He has remembered* ("zachar") *His lovingkindness.* G-d's attribute of lovingkindness is "*zachar*"—"masculine." Awe, however, is a more feminine trait, as in the verse (Proverbs 13:30), *A G-d-fearing woman* (see *Tanya*, ch. 43; *Torah Or*, ibid.). Perhaps this is related to the masculine role of "giver" and the characteristically feminine trait of "recipient." Lovingkindness typifies a "giver," whereas the nature of a "recipient, to take and hold within" is characteristic of discipline and awe.

ח.

וּלְבָאֵר אֹפֶן הָעֲבוֹדָה דְוַעֲבַדְתֶּם אֵת הוי׳ אֱלֹקֵיכֶם, מַמְשִׁיךְ בַּכָּתוּב לֹא תִהְיֶה מְשַׁכֵּלָה וַעֲקָרָה גו׳.

דְּהִנֵּה[נג], עֲקָרָה הִיא שֶׁאֵינָהּ יוֹלֶדֶת בָּנִים, דְּקָאֵי עַל הַמִּדּוֹת אַהֲבָה וְיִרְאָה (תּוֹלְדוֹת הַהִתְבּוֹנְנוּת[נד]), שֶׁאַהֲבָה הִיא בְּחִינַת בֵּן וְיִרְאָה הִיא בְּחִינַת בַּת.

וּמְשַׁכֵּלָה הִיא שֶׁיּוֹלֶדֶת אַהֲבָה וְיִרְאָה, אֶלָּא שֶׁאֵין לָהֶם קִיּוּם.

וְעַל זֶה בָּא הַצִּוּוּי לֹא תִהְיֶה מְשַׁכֵּלָה וַעֲקָרָה, שֶׁהַהִתְבּוֹנְנוּת צְרִיכָה לִהְיוֹת בְּאֹפֶן שֶׁתִּהְיֶה מִזֶּה הוֹלָדַת הַמִּדּוֹת, וְהַמִּדּוֹת יִהְיוּ בְּקִיּוּם, שֶׁאָז תִּהְיֶה הָעֲבוֹדָה דְוַעֲבַדְתֶּם אֵת הוי׳ אֱלֹקֵיכֶם כִּדְבָעֵי.

וּבֵאוּר הָעִנְיָן[נה],

הִנֵּה, בַּעֲקָרָה שֶׁאֵינָהּ יוֹלֶדֶת יֵשׁ ב׳ בְּחִינוֹת. בְּחִינָה הָא׳, שֶׁאֲפִילוּ בֵּית וָלָד (בֵּית מַטְרוֹן[נו]) אֵין לָהּ[נז], הַיְינוּ, שֶׁאֵין לָהּ כְּלִי קִבּוּל לְקַבֵּל הַהֵרָיוֹן לְצֹרֶךְ הַלֵּדָה. וְעִנְיָנוֹ בַּעֲבוֹדָה, שֶׁבֵּית וָלָד קָאֵי עַל הַהִתְפַּעֲלוּת שִׂכְלִית שֶׁעַל יָדָהּ תִּהְיֶה הוֹלָדַת הַמִּדּוֹת בְּהִתְגַּלּוּת לִבּוֹ, וַעֲקָרָה

92. See *Torah Or*, ibid.; *Torat Chaim*, ibid., p. 432a [297a—ed. 2003] ff.; *Or Hatorah*, ibid.

93. As was the case at first with the matriarchs Sara and Rebecca—see *Yevamot* 64b; *Bereshit Rabbah* 47:2; 53:5; 63:5. Cited also in *Or Hachaim* on Genesis 21:2.

94. For the connection between the womb and intellect see *Tanya*, ch. 3: "The intellect of the rational soul, which is the faculty that conceives any thing, is given the appellation of *chochmah*.... When one brings forth this power from the potential into the actual, that is, when a person cogitates with his intellect in order to understand a thing truly and profoundly as it evolves from the concept which he has conceived in his intellect, this is called *binah*. *Chochmah* and *binah* are the very 'father' and 'mother' which give birth to love of G-d, and awe and dread of Him. For when the intellect in the rational soul deeply contemplates...the greatness of G-d,

who lacks a womb" in the service of G-d corresponds to a situation in which not only is there an absence of love and awe revealed within the heart—a result of *timtum halev*—but there is not even any intellectual excitement, a result of *timtum hamoach.*[95]

A FILLED VESSEL

The cause for absence is that the person is not receptive when he is a "full vessel," for naturally, "a full vessel cannot contain."[96] When a person is a full vessel, i.e., completely occupied with his own personal wishes [he cannot feel spiritual emptiness].

WHETHER WITH EVIL OR WITH THE HOLY

This is not necessarily because of the desires of his evil inclination that seeks the forbidden, or even to the wishes of the animal soul that desires what is permissible—for although they are permissible, the desire for them is at least "a demon of a Jewish nature."[97] But even with regards to the wishes of his G-dly soul, namely, holy desires—if he is full of and involved with his personal desires, convincing himself that he is capable of a specific divine service, and therefore wants to engage in it particularly but not in another—then he is "a full vessel that cannot contain." He is incapable of grasping the truth within his mind for it to lead to intellectual excitement.

---

how He fills...and encompasses all worlds, and in the presence of Whom everything is considered as nothing—there will be born...in his mind and thought the emotion of awe for the divine majesty.... Next, his heart will glow with an intense love..., with a passion, desire and longing..., towards the greatness of the blessed *Ein Sof.*"

95. TIMTUM HALEV (lit., "dullness of the heart") and TIMTUM HAMOACH (lit., "dullness of the mind") are states in which one's heart and mind are dulled to spiritual excitement. Indifference and lack of interest are characteristics of a dull mind, whereas the resistance to transforming intellectual excitement into heartfelt emotion is a sign of a dull heart. These two states of dullness are symptoms of being overly engrossed in earthly and materialistic pursuits. See *Tanya*, ch. 29; *Likkutei Torah, Chukat* 66c.

96. *Berachot* 40a. In order for a person to develop an interest in spiritual-

שֶׁאֵין לָהּ בֵּית וָלָד פֵּרוּשׁוֹ, שֶׁלֹּא זוֹ בִּלְבָד שֶׁאֵין לוֹ אַהֲבָה וְיִרְאָה בְּהִתְגַּלּוּת לִבּוֹ, שֶׁזֶּהוּ עִנְיַן טִמְטוּם הַלֵּב, אֶלָּא שֶׁאֵין לוֹ אֲפִילוּ הִתְפַּעֲלוּת שִׂכְלִית, שֶׁזֶּהוּ עִנְיַן טִמְטוּם הַמּוֹחַ.

וְהַסִּבָּה לָזֶה הִיא מִפְּנֵי שֶׁאֵינוֹ כְּלִי קִבּוּל, לִהְיוֹתוֹ כְּלִי מָלֵא, וּבְמִדַּת בָּשָׂר וָדָם כְּלִי מָלֵא אֵינוֹ מַחֲזִיק[נח]. דְּהִנֵּה, כַּאֲשֶׁר הָאָדָם הוּא כְּלִי מָלֵא, הַיְינוּ, שֶׁהוּא מָלֵא מֵהָרְצוֹנוֹת שֶׁלּוֹ

לֹא מִבָּעֵי רְצוֹנוֹת דְּיֵצֶר הָרָע, שֶׁהֵם הָרְצוֹנוֹת לִדְבָרִים הָאֲסוּרִים, אוֹ אֲפִילוּ רְצוֹנוֹת דְּנֶפֶשׁ הַבַּהֲמִית לִדְבָרִים הַמֻּתָּרִים, דְּעִם הֱיוֹתָם דְּבָרִים מֻתָּרִים, הֲרֵי הַתַּאֲוָה אֲלֵיהֶם הִיא בְּחִינַת שֵׁד מְשֵׁדִין יְהוּדָאִין עַל כָּל פָּנִים[נט], אֶלָּא אֲפִילוּ רְצוֹנוֹת דְּנֶפֶשׁ הָאֱלֹקִית, הַיְינוּ רְצוֹנוֹת דִּקְדֻשָּׁה, הִנֵּה אִם הוּא מָלֵא וְעָסוּק בְּהָרְצוֹנוֹת שֶׁלּוֹ, לוֹמַר שֶׁעֲבוֹדָה זוֹ יֵשׁ לוֹ חוּשׁ בָּהּ כו', עֲבוֹדָה זוֹ הוּא רוֹצֶה וַעֲבוֹדָה זוֹ אֵינוֹ רוֹצֶה (דִּי עֲבוֹדָה ווִיל עֶר אוּן דִּי עֲבוֹדָה ווִיל עֶר נִיט), אַזֵי הוּא כְּלִי מָלֵא שֶׁאֵינוֹ מַחֲזִיק, שֶׁאֵינוֹ תּוֹפֵס הָאֱמֶת בְּמוֹחוֹ וְשִׂכְלוֹ לִהְיוֹת מִזֶּה הִתְפַּעֲלוּת שִׂכְלִית.

---

ity, he must first feel a sense of emptiness—i.e., that he is lacking in his spirituality. This feeling creates a vacuum-like urge that excites the person to fill that void and become interested in spirituality. This cannot be accomplished when the person is a "full vessel," focused solely upon filling his own wishes and desires. Hence the first meaning of "barren" presented here in divine service.

97. *Tanya*, ch. 8 (13a) citing *Zohar* III:253a; 277a.

DEMONS OF A JEWISH NATURE. In Kabbalistic terminology, the evil inclination is called a "demon" because it lures the person away from serving G-d. Even when one desires to partake of something permissible, if the desire is without G-dly purpose, it emanates from the evil inclination and is considered a demon, albeit of a Jewish nature (for the thing is permissible). See *Mekor Mayim Chaim* to *Baal Shem Tov Al Hatorah*, *Korach*, fn. 5.

NO BIRTH

The second type of barren woman has a womb yet does not give birth. This refers to a person who has a "womb" with which to comprehend and become intellectually excited, but no emotions are born from this excitement to be revealed within the heart:

QUINTESSENTIAL TREMOR

Just as physical childbirth requires an impregnation assisted by the revelation of the power of the *Ein Sof*,[98] giving birth to emotions also requires an impregnation, *a light [that] is sown for the righteous*,[99] which refers to sowing the seeds of Torah and *mitzvot*,[100] that is accomplished specifically by way of a supernal power. This is the "quintessential tremor"[101] that transcends logic and reason that must be experienced at least once a year, at the start of the service of G-d.

Even after the impregnation, there is the gestation period in which the fetus gradually grows until it is born into the world. Similarly, there is a gestation period to give birth to emotions that become revealed within the heart.[102]

---

98. See *Likkutei Torah*, *Shir Hashirim* 39d ff.; *Sefer Hamaamarim 5652* p. 130 ff.; *5657* p. 179 ff.

99. Psalms 97:11. See following note.

100. PLANTING TORAH AND MITZVOT. Studying Torah and performing *mitzvot* are similar to planting in the sense that one needs only to perform the deed and the infinite divine light becomes channeled on its own. As in literal planting, the transformation of a tiny, lifeless seed into a large and fruitful tree is a truly miraculous manifestation of the divine and infinite creative power. The orchardist only prepares the resources for the growth, but it is G-d who causes it to actually grow. Similarly, when one fulfills G-d's will by studying Torah or performing a mitzvah, one "plants the seeds," i.e., sets the stage for infinite divine light to be channeled into the world.

Hence the verse *Light is sown for the righteous*: their Torah study and performance of *mitzvot* causes divine light to descend and to be sown into this world, in a hidden manner, like a seed hidden in the earth. The effect of this Torah study and mitzvah performance will be revealed only in the Messianic era, just as plants sprout up from their earthly concealment. See *Torah Or*, *Vayechi* 54c.

וְעִנְיָן הַב' בַּעֲקָרָה, שֶׁיֵּשׁ לָהּ בֵּית וָלָד, אֶלָּא שֶׁאֵינָהּ יוֹלֶדֶת, וְהַיְינוּ שֶׁיֵּשׁ לוֹ כְּלִי קִבּוּל לֵידַע וּלְהִתְפָּעֵל בְּשִׂכְלוֹ, אֶלָּא שֶׁלֹּא נַעֲשָׂה מִזֶּה הוֹלָדַת הַמִּדּוֹת בְּהִתְגַּלּוּת לִבּוֹ.

דְּהִנֵּה, כְּשֵׁם שֶׁלְּצֹרֶךְ הַהוֹלָדָה בְּגַשְׁמִיּוּת צָרִיךְ לִהְיוֹת עִנְיַן הַזְּרִיעָה עַל יְדֵי גִלּוּי כֹּחַ הָאֵין סוֹף[ס], כְּמוֹ כֵן לְצֹרֶךְ הוֹלָדַת הַמִּדּוֹת צָרִיךְ לִהְיוֹת עִנְיַן הַזְּרִיעָה, אוֹר זָרוּעַ לַצַּדִּיק[סא], דְּקָאֵי עַל הַזְּרִיעָה דְתוֹרָה וּמִצְוֹת, וּבָא עַל יְדֵי כֹּחַ עֶלְיוֹן דַּוְקָא, שֶׁזּוֹהִי הַהֲזָזָה עַצְמִית שֶׁלְּמַעְלָה מִטַּעַם וָדַעַת שֶׁצְּרִיכָה לִהְיוֹת לְכָל הַפָּחוֹת פַּעַם אַחַת בַּשָּׁנָה, בְּהַתְחָלַת הָעֲבוֹדָה[סב].

וְגַם לְאַחֲרֵי הַזְּרִיעָה יֶשְׁנוֹ הַסֵּדֶר דִּימֵי הָעִבּוּר, שֶׁהַוָּלָד הוֹלֵךְ וְגָדֵל כו' עַד שֶׁמִּתְגַּלֶּה בַּאֲוִיר הָעוֹלָם, וּכְמוֹ כֵן יֶשְׁנוֹ גַּם הַסֵּדֶר דִּימֵי הָעִבּוּר כו' לְצֹרֶךְ לֵדַת הַמִּדּוֹת בְּהִתְגַּלּוּת הַלֵּב[סג].

---

101. HAZAZAH ATZMIT, in the Hebrew, is the experience of being spiritually inspired and moved to the core of one's soul. During the High Holidays, when G-d's presence is felt in a stronger manner, it is the time to awaken a quintessential tremor that lays the foundation for a renewed service of G-d in the New Year. (See *Sefer Hamaamarim 5703*, p. 19.) The quintessential tremor results from both human effort and divine assistance. Because G-d makes Himself more readily available at that time, it is easier for the person to access G-dliness by way of his own effort. Although he must still plant the seeds, what he reaps is far greater than what his effort is capable of accomplishing, due to the divine presence that comes to his assistance and enables him to experience the quintessential tremor.

102. See *Torat Chaim*, *Beshalach* 161b ff. [*Bo* 129a—ed. 2003]. In the second type of "barrenness," this impregnation is absent, and therefore, although there is a womb, it does not give birth. The chapter concludes that once one has achieved not being "barren," i.e., there is a) a womb and b) an active one, with impregnation, care must be taken that the "pregnancy" last and give birth to love and awe.

“NONE SHALL MISCARRY...”

However, even once the emotions of love and awe are born and become revealed in the heart (the opposite of *barrenness*), care must be taken that they should be viable (the opposite of *miscarriage*). Only then [does it become apparent that] the service of G-d is true, as the verse states, *The lip of truth shall be established forever.*[103]

9.

SPIRITUAL CONTENTMENT

It is also important for one to find a way not to [become content with one’s *avodah*].[104]

This applies even when one serves G-d in a suitable manner, with both intellectual comprehension and emotions of the heart that are revealed within his heart and which are not merely false impressions but true love and awe that are recognizable through his adherence to Torah and *mitzvot.*

In addition to actually observing Torah and *mitzvot*, he is also aware of the meaning of the *mitzvot* and is even aware of the divine revelations that the performance of *mitzvot* elicit. [For example, giving charity elicits a spiritual revelation in the path of *chesed*, lovingkindness; serving G-d in matters of discipline—[as exemplified by the verse] *You have made judgment...in Jacob*[105]—elicits a spiritual revelation in the path of *gevurah*, discipline; Torah study, which is the middle path, elicits a revelation that is [likewise] in the middle path.[106]]

---

103. Proverbs 12:19. *The lip of truth*—when the truth is spoken, it is *established forever*—it is everlasting. In contrast, the verse continues, *But a lying tongue is but for a moment*—i.e., falsehood does not last. When the emotions of love and awe do not dissipate but remain for a long time, it is a sign that they were truthful to begin with. See *Tanya*, ch. 13.

104. When a person is satisfied with his current state, he loses his ambition to invest effort and apply himself to furthering his current state, as will be explained below.

105. Psalms 99:4. *Judgment...in Jacob* refers to the laws of Torah that guide Jacob. *You have made* emphasizes that G-d established these laws. See *Metzudat David* on the verse. In par-

אָמְנָם, גַּם לְאַחֲרֵי שֶׁנּוֹלְדוּ הַמִּדּוֹת דְּאַהֲבָה וְיִרְאָה בְּהִתְגַּלּוּת לִבּוֹ (הַשְּׁלִילָה דַּעֲקָרָה), צְרִיכָה לִהְיוֹת הַזְּהִירוּת שֶׁיִּהְיֶה לָהֶם קִיּוּם (הַשְּׁלִילָה דִּמְשַׁכֶּלָה), שֶׁדַּוְקָא אָז הָעֲבוֹדָה הִיא אֲמִתִּית, כְּמוֹ שֶׁכָּתוּב[סד] שְׂפַת אֱמֶת תִּכּוֹן לָעַד.

ט.

אַךְ עוֹד אַחַת צָרִיךְ לָשִׁית עֵצוֹת בְּנַפְשׁוֹ,

שֶׁגַּם כַּאֲשֶׁר עוֹבֵד עֲבוֹדָתוֹ כִּדְבָעֵי, הֵן בְּנוֹגֵעַ לְהַשָּׂגָה שֶׁבַּמּוֹחַ, וְהֵן בְּנוֹגֵעַ לְהַמִּדּוֹת שֶׁבַּלֵּב, שֶׁהֵם בְּהִתְגַּלּוּת לִבּוֹ, וְאֵינָם דִּמְיוֹנוֹת שָׁוְא, אֶלָּא אַהֲבָה וְיִרְאָה אֲמִתִּיִּים, וְנִרְגָּשִׁים גַּם בְּקִיּוּם הַתּוֹרָה וּמִצְווֹת,

שֶׁנּוֹסָף עַל קִיּוּם הַתּוֹרָה וּמִצְווֹת בְּפֹעַל מַמָּשׁ, יוֹדֵעַ הוּא כַּוָּנַת הַמִּצְווֹת, וְיוֹדֵעַ גַּם הַהַמְשָׁכוֹת שֶׁנַּעֲשׂוֹת עַל יְדֵי קִיּוּם הַמִּצְווֹת [שֶׁעַל יְדֵי עֲבוֹדַת הַצְּדָקָה הַהַמְשָׁכָה הִיא בְּקַו הַחֶסֶד, וְעַל יְדֵי עֲבוֹדַת הַגְּבוּרָה, מִשְׁפָּט גו' בְּיַעֲקֹב[סה], נַעֲשֵׂית הַהַמְשָׁכָה בְּקַו הַגְּבוּרָה, וְעַל יְדֵי לִמּוּד הַתּוֹרָה, שֶׁהוּא קַו הָאֶמְצָעִי, נַעֲשֵׂית הַהַמְשָׁכָה בְּקַו הָאֶמְצָעִי],

---

ticular, this verse refers to restricting one's involvement in prohibited, unholy, and superfluous activities.

All evil receives nurture from *gevurah* (the supernal aspect of discipline), since only by limiting the Infinite can there be room for any opposition. Serving G-d by way of restriction elicits *gevurah*, and ensures that it is not channeled to nurture evil, but rather that its restrictive nature works to exclude evil. See *Torah Or, Beshalach* 63b.

106. THREE PATHS. In Kabbalah, "path" (*kav*, in Hebrew) refers to the direction of divine influx as it is channeled through the spiritual worlds. The *middot* (divine emotive attributes) are divided into three paths. The path on the right is the path of *chesed*, which includes the *middot* of

He may have even reached the point where his service of G-d fulfills the level that is alluded to in the specific wording of the verse, *And you shall serve Havaya your Elokim*, i.e., that as a result of your serving G-d, the name *Havaya*, representing "past, present, and future" as one—and at an even higher level, the aspect of *Havaya* as it transcends *hishtalshelut*—becomes your *Elokim*, your energy and life-force.[107]

STUNTED PROGRESS

Even when a person has attained this state of spiritual elevation, he should be mindful not to become satisfied with his service of G-d, for then he is arrested in his current state and does not continue to progress in his service of G-d: In addition to the possibility that the feeling of satisfaction could stunt the continuity of his existing love and awe that are already born and revealed (i.e., the concept of *miscarriage*)—while engaging in divine service with love and awe, his service remains limited and confined to what is required for his satisfaction.[108]

ASPIRATIONS

Regarding this the verse states, *None shall miscarry or be barren* in your land—specifically *in your* ***land***. The Hebrew word *eretz*, land, is related to the word *ratzon*, will.[109] The verse means that the ideal servant does not even feel satisfaction

---

chesed and *netzach* (lovingkindness and endurance). The left path is the path of *gevurah*, which includes the *middot* of *gevurah* and *hod* (discipline and glory). The middle path is the path of *tiferet*, which includes the *middot* of *tiferet*, *yesod*, and *malchut* (harmony, bonding, and sovereignty). Torah relates to the middle path, the path of harmony and truth, as explained in fn. 57.

107. HAVAYA BECOMES YOUR ELOKIM. G-d's name *Havaya* (see fn. 45) represents G-dliness as it transcends the worlds. This is indicated in the word *Havaya*, an acronym for the words *hayah* (past), *hoveh* (present), and *yihiyeh* (future)—i.e., *Havaya* is a state of G-dliness that transcends the worldly divisions of time. Chasidus teaches that from the perspective of *Havaya*, the world is not considered an entity and is as if it does not exist. The service of G-d to become aware of G-dliness and to awaken an emotional love and awe is meant to be done to the degree that "*Havaya* be-

וְעַד שֶׁעֲבוֹדָתוֹ הִיא בְּאֹפֶן הַמְּרֻמָּז בְּדִיּוּק לְשׁוֹן הַכָּתוּב וַעֲבַדְתֶּם אֵת הוי' אֱלֹקֵיכֶם, שֶׁשֵּׁם הוי', הָיָה הֹוֶה וְיִהְיֶה כְּאֶחָד, וּלְמַעְלָה יוֹתֵר בְּחִינַת הוי' שֶׁלְּמַעְלָה מֵהִשְׁתַּלְשְׁלוּת, נַעֲשֶׂה אֱלֹקֵיכֶם, כֹּחֲכֶם וְחַיּוּתְכֶם[סו],

הִנֵּה גַּם בִּהְיוֹתוֹ בְּמַעֲמָד וּמַצָּב כָּזֶה, צָרִיךְ לְהִזָּהֵר שֶׁלֹּא תִהְיֶה לוֹ שְׂבִיעוּת רָצוֹן מֵעֲבוֹדָתוֹ, שֶׁאָז נִשְׁאָר לַעֲמוֹד עַל עָמְדוֹ וְאֵינוֹ מוֹסִיף לְהַלֵּךְ בַּעֲבוֹדָתוֹ (עֶר שְׁטֶעלְט זִיךְ אָפּ אוּן גֵייט נִיט וַוייטֶער). כִּי, נוֹסָף לָזֶה שֶׁהֶרְגֵּשׁ דִּשְׂבִיעוּת רָצוֹן יָכוֹל לִגְרוֹם לְכַךְ שֶׁהָאַהֲבָה וְיִרְאָה שֶׁכְּבָר נוֹלְדוּ וְנִתְגַּלּוּ לֹא יִהְיוּ בְּקִיּוּמָם (שֶׁזֶּהוּ עִנְיָן דִּמְשַׁכֵּלָה), הִנֵּה גַּם בְּשָׁעָה שֶׁעוֹבֵד עֲבוֹדָתוֹ בְּאַהֲבָה וְיִרְאָה, תִּהְיֶה עֲבוֹדָתוֹ בִּמְדִידָה וְהַגְבָּלָה, בְּמִדָּה הַנִּדְרֶשֶׁת מִשְּׂבִיעוּת הָרָצוֹן שֶׁלּוֹ[סז].

וְעַל זֶה נֶאֱמַר לֹא תִהְיֶה מְשַׁכֵּלָה וַעֲקָרָה בְּאַרְצֶךָ[ד], בְּאַרְצֶךָ דַּיְקָא, שֶׁאֶרֶץ הוּא מִלְּשׁוֹן רָצוֹן[סח], הַיְינוּ, שֶׁלֹּא יֻרְגַּשׁ אֶצְלוֹ אֲפִילוּ שְׂבִיעוּת רָצוֹן בִּלְבַד מֵעֲבוֹדָתוֹ

---

comes your *Elokim*." Literally, *Elokim* means "mighty ones," connoting strength, energy, and power. *Elokim* is the name of G-d that represents His appearance within nature and corporeality. Therefore, serving G-d to the degree that "*Havaya* becomes your *Elokim*" means to instill an awareness of G-d's transcendence and the negligibility of worldliness (*Havaya*) into one's mind and heart to the point that he knows G-d is his reality, his energy, and his life-force (*Elokim*). See *Torah Or*, ibid., 79a; *Torat Chaim*, *Mishpatim* 431b [296d—ed. 2003]; *Or Hatorah*, ibid., p. 1255.

108. See *Torah Or*, ibid., 78d; *Torat Chaim*, ibid., 431a [296d—ed. 2003]; *Or Hatorah*, ibid.

109. See *Bereshit Rabbah* 5:8 and *Matnot Kehunah*, there, that at the time of creation, G-d named the dry surface of the earth "*eretz*" (Genesis 1:10) for its association with the word "*ratzon*," (will)—"for it 'wanted' to fulfill the will of its master."

(i.e., the fulfillment of his will) from his service of G-d. (He certainly does not feel his own wishes, since that would make him a full vessel that cannot contain, i.e., he would have no receptacle [i.e., no womb to receive impregnation] at all—the first form of barrenness that was mentioned earlier.)

10.

LIMITED TIME

The verse continues: *The number of your days I will fill.*[110]

This is the advice that the Torah offers for developing feelings of inner discontent.

When one contemplates that he is given a set number of days [to live]—*The days in which they are to be fashioned*[111]—no less and no more, and that on every day, every hour, and at every moment, he must labor to fulfill his mission in this world—it troubles him so much that he has no time at all to think about [lofty] aspirations.

NO TIME TO THINK

This is similar to the words of Rabban Yochanan Ben Zakkai, "I do not know by which path I will be taken."[112] One of the meanings of this statement is that he was so involved in fulfilling his mission that he did not have any time to focus on his personal aspirations.[113]

The person is so concerned with and immersed ("pressed, pressured, and overwhelmed"[114]) in fulfilling his mission every

---

110. Regarding the following—see *Torah Or*, *Mishpatim* 79b ff.; *Torat Chaim*, ibid., 437a ff.; *Or Hatorah*, ibid., p. 1261 ff.; *Sefer Hamaamarim 5692*, p. 223.

111. Psalms 139:16. The literal meaning of the verse is that a specific amount of days are created for each individual. According to the interpretation of the *Zohar* (I:224a) and Chasidus, the days themselves are to be fashioned. In addition to fulfilling everything that is required, one must also ensure that he is involved in the service of G-d at all times. Thus, one must fashion his days by filling all of his days, hours, and minutes with the service of G-d. (*Torah Or*, ibid.; *Torat Chaim*, ibid., 437b ff.; *Or Hatorah*, ibid.; see also *Vayedaber... Va'erah, 5712*, and *V'Avraham Zaken, 5738*.)

112. *Berachot* 28b: "When Rabban

(וּפְשִׁיטָא שֶׁלֹּא יִהְיוּ נִרְגָּשִׁים הָרְצוֹנוֹת שֶׁלּוֹ, שֶׁאָז הוּא כְּלִי מָלֵא שֶׁאֵינוֹ מַחֲזִיק, שֶׁאֵין לוֹ בֵּית קִבּוּל כְּלָל, בְּחִינָה הָא' דַּעֲקָרָה הַנַּ"ל).

י.

וּמַמְשִׁיךְ בַּכָּתוּב אֶת מִסְפַּר יָמֶיךָ אֲמַלֵּא[סט],

שֶׁזּוֹהִי הָעֵצָה הַיְעוּצָה כְּדֵי לִפְעוֹל בְּנַפְשׁוֹ הֶרְגֵּשׁ שֶׁל הֶעְדֵּר שְׂבִיעוּת הָרָצוֹן.

וְהָעִנְיָן בָּזֶה, שֶׁכַּאֲשֶׁר הָאָדָם מִתְבּוֹנֵן שֶׁנִּתְּנוּ לוֹ יָמִים קְצוּבִים, יָמִים יֻצָּרוּ גו'[ע], לֹא פָּחוֹת וְלֹא יוֹתֵר, וּבְכָל יוֹם, בְּכָל שָׁעָה וּבְכָל רֶגַע צָרִיךְ לַעֲבוֹד עֲבוֹדָתוֹ לְמַלֵּא שְׁלִיחוּתוֹ בְּעָלְמָא דֵין, הֲרֵי הוּא טָרוּד בָּזֶה כָּל כַּךְ עַד שֶׁאֵין לוֹ פְּנַאי כְּלָל לַחְשׁוֹב אוֹדוֹת עִנְיָנִים שֶׁל מַדְרֵגוֹת.

וְעַל דֶּרֶךְ מַאֲמַר רַבָּן יוֹחָנָן בֶּן זַכַּאי[עא] אֵינִי יוֹדֵעַ בְּאֵיזוֹ דֶּרֶךְ מוֹלִיכִין אוֹתִי, וּמֵהַבֵּאוּרִים בָּזֶה[עב], שֶׁמִּצַּד גֹּדֶל טִרְדָּתוֹ בְּמִלּוּי שְׁלִיחוּתוֹ לֹא הָיָה לוֹ פְּנַאי לָשִׂים לֵב (צוּהֶערְן זִיךְ) לְמַדְרֵגוֹת שֶׁלּוֹ[עג].

וְהַיְינוּ, שֶׁהוּא טָרוּד וְשָׁקוּעַ כָּל כַּךְ (עֶר אִיז אַזוֹי פִיל פַארִיאָגְט, פַארַאֵיינְגְט אוּן פַארְטְרוּנְקֶען) בְּמִלּוּי

Yochanan ben Zakkai fell ill, his disciples went in to visit him. When he saw them, he began to weep. His disciples said to him, 'Lamp of Israel, pillar of the right hand, mighty hammer! Why do you weep?' He replied, '...When there are two ways before me, one leading to *Gan Eden* and the other to *Gehenom*, and I do not know by which I will be taken, should I not weep?'" The discourse proceeds to provide one explanation of Rabban Yochanan's statement. (For alternate explanations, see *Maamarei Admur Hazaken Haketzarim*, p. 309; *Or Hatorah*, *Pinchas*, p. 1059 ff.; *Torat Shmuel—Sefer 5626*, p. 171 ff.; *5646*, p. 14 ff.; *5696*, p. 50 ff.)

113. See *Kitzurim V'he'arot L'tanya*, p. 47.

114. These parenthetical remarks appear in the original transcript, in Yiddish: עֶר אִיז אַזוֹי פִיל פַארִיאָגְט, פַארַאֵיינְגְט אוּן פַארְטְרוּנְקֶען.

day, every hour, and at every moment that he is not aware of the state of his intellect and emotions, and certainly not the hidden aspects of his soul.[115]

REBELLING AGAINST THE KING

It is understood from this, *a fortiori*, that there is certainly no room to feel spiritually satisfied.

For when a person knows that at every moment he must fulfill his mission [in life], and if one moment passes in which he does not fulfill his mission, not only does he miss out on an opportunity to advance and flourish in his service of G-d,[116] but, moreover, at that moment he rebels[117] against the King, King of Kings, the Holy One blessed be He, by the mere fact that he is not fulfilling His mission—then, not only is he beyond feeling satisfaction—as the verse stated, *in your land*, [i.e., *your aspirations*]—but on the contrary, when he is asked "What is the status of your *be'artzecha*?" he cries out bitterly "What have I with [holy] desires! What have I with delight? What have I with love [of G-d]? What have I with awe?[118] How could I think about aspirations when I need to stand on guard constantly not to let even one moment pass in a state of rebellion against the king, heaven forbid, by not fulfilling His mission at that moment?!"[119]

---

115. See *Vayikach Hashem Elokim, 5712*; *Bereshit Bara, 5713*.

116. In the original transcript, this appears in Yiddish: עֶר הָאט גֶעקֶענְט שְׁטַייגְן.

117. At this point, while delivering the discourse, the Rebbe broke down in tears and placed his head on the table. After several moments the Rebbe resumed the discourse.

118. In the original transcript, this appears in Yiddish: שְׁרַייט עֶר אוֹיס . . . וואָס מִיר רָצוֹן, וואָס מִיר תַּעֲנוּג, וואָס מִיר אַהֲבָה, וואָס מִיר יִרְאָה.

119. This does not mean that the service of G-d should be accomplished in a constant state of bitterness and awe. Even Rabban Yochanan ben Zakkai spent his entire life serving G-d in a state of joy. Only during his

שְׁלִיחוּתוֹ בְּכָל יוֹם וּבְכָל שָׁעָה וּבְכָל רֶגַע, שֶׁאֵינוֹ יוֹדֵעַ מַה נַּעֲשֶׂה עִם שִׂכְלוֹ וּמִדּוֹתָיו, וְעַל אַחַת כַּמָּה וְכַמָּה בַּנּוֹגֵעַ לְמַדְרֵגוֹת הַנֶּעְלָמוֹת שֶׁבַּנֶּפֶשׁ[עד].

וּמִזֶּה מוּבָן בְּמִכָּל שֶׁכֵּן וְקַל וָחֹמֶר שֶׁלֹּא שַׁיָּךְ אֶצְלוֹ רֶגֶשׁ שֶׁל שְׂבִיעוּת רָצוֹן,

כִּי, בְּיָדְעוֹ שֶׁבְּכָל רֶגַע וָרֶגַע צָרִיךְ לְמַלֵּא אֶת שְׁלִיחוּתוֹ, וְאִם עוֹבֵר רֶגַע שֶׁאֵינוֹ עוֹבֵד עֲבוֹדָתוֹ, הֲרֵי זֶה לֹא רַק שֶׁהָיָה יָכוֹל לְהִתְעַלּוֹת וּלְשַׂגְשֵׂג בַּעֲבוֹדָתוֹ (עֶר הָאט גֶעקֶענְט שְׁטַייגְן) וְלֹא עָשָׂה כֵּן, אֶלָּא עוֹד זֹאת, שֶׁבְּרֶגַע זֶה שֶׁאֵינוֹ עוֹבֵד עֲבוֹדָתוֹ, מוֹרֵד[עה] הוּא בְּמֶלֶךְ מַלְכֵי הַמְּלָכִים הַקָּדוֹשׁ בָּרוּךְ הוּא בְּכַךְ שֶׁאֵינוֹ מְמַלֵּא אֶת שְׁלִיחוּתוֹ, הֲרֵי, לֹא זוֹ בִּלְבָד שֶׁלֹּא שַׁיָּךְ אֶצְלוֹ הֶרְגֵּשׁ שֶׁל שְׂבִיעוּת רָצוֹן, בְּאַרְצֶךָ, אֶלָּא אַדְּרַבָּה, וֶוען מֶען פְרֶעגְט אִים וואָס אִיז בַּאַ דִיר מִיטְן בְּאַרְצֶךָ, זוֹעֵק הוּא (שְׁרַייט עֶר אוֹיס) בְּמַר נַפְשׁוֹ: מַה לִּי רָצוֹן, מַה לִּי תַּעֲנוּג, מַה לִּי אַהֲבָה, מַה לִּי יִרְאָה (וואָס מִיר רָצוֹן, וואָס מִיר תַּעֲנוּג, וואָס מִיר אַהֲבָה, וואָס מִיר יִרְאָה), כֵּיצַד יָכוֹל לַחְשׁוֹב עַל עִנְיָנִים שֶׁל מַדְרֵגוֹת בָּהּ בְּשָׁעָה שֶׁצָּרִיךְ לַעֲמוֹד עַל הַמִּשְׁמָר שֶׁלֹּא יַעֲבוֹר אֲפִילוּ רֶגַע אֶחָד בְּמַצָּב שֶׁל מְרִידָה בְּמַלְכוּת חַס וְשָׁלוֹם מִצַּד הַחִסָּרוֹן בְּמִלּוּי הַשְּׁלִיחוּת בְּרֶגַע זֶה.

---

final moments, when he was to be led down one of the two paths, did he weep bitterly over the state of his soul. See *Kitzurim V'ha'arot L'tanya*, ibid.

To summarize: The verse had stated that one is not to feel satisfied with his *avodah*. However, it is actually needless to give such instruction, for if at every moment one is pressed to complete one's mission, then he does not even stand a chance to give any thought to any aspirations at all, let alone satisfaction! Having presented these thoughts, the discourse continues by providing reassurance.

11.

G-D'S PART

When a person fulfills the instruction that *None shall miscarry or be barren*—i.e., he does everything in his power to ensure that his service of G-d is from true love and awe that will be viable, and with discontent [over his spiritual state]—then, G-d will add to his efforts and will guarantee that in fact *None* shall *miscarry or be barren* (here, an expression of assurance) *in your land.*[120]

12.

In this light, we can further elucidate the verse, *The number of your days I will fill.* (In addition to the person's contemplation about the number of days allotted to him,) the verse specifically states, ***I** will fill*—meaning, G-d. Furthermore, this is stated in the first person, to refer to the Narrator of the Torah Himself, the actual essence of the *Ein Sof* blessed be He, who transcends *hishtalshelut* (as mentioned earlier).

SPARKLING DAYS

Even when a person lacks in the "number of days" in which he served G-d (i.e., he had days in which he did not fulfill his mission or even days in which he did what he should not have done), nevertheless, because the Narrator of the Torah transcends *hishtalshelut*—a level at which there can be no defect—the [defects in] number of days allotted to him are filled. And even more than what was allotted: all the days become "full,"[121] not only as full days, but also splendorous days. This explains the emphasis of the verse, *the number* (mispar) *of your days.*[122] The Hebrew word for number, *mispar*, is related to the word *mesaprim*, as in the verse,[123] *The heavens* mesaprim (lit.,—*declare,* fig.—radiate), i.e., they

---

120. There is a short segment missing at this point in the transcript of the discourse.

121. See *Torat Chaim*, ibid., 439b ff. See *Or Hatorah*, *Mishpatim* p. 1266; ibid. (vol. 7), p. 2731.

יא.

וְהִנֵּה כַּאֲשֶׁר הָאָדָם מְקַיֵּם הַצִּוּוּי לֹא תִהְיֶה מְשַׁכֵּלָה וַעֲקָרָה בְּאַרְצֶךָ, שֶׁעוֹשֶׂה כָּל אֲשֶׁר בִּיכָלְתּוֹ שֶׁתִּהְיֶה עֲבוֹדָתוֹ בְּאַהֲבָה וְיִרְאָה אֲמִתִּיִּים שֶׁיֵּשׁ לָהֶם קִיּוּם, וּמִתּוֹךְ הֶעְדֵּר שְׂבִיעוּת רָצוֹן כו׳ כַּנַ״ל, אֲזַי מוֹסִיפִים וּמַבְטִיחִים לוֹ מִלְמַעְלָה שֶׁלֹּא תִהְיֶה (בִּלְשׁוֹן הַבְטָחָה) מְשַׁכֵּלָה וַעֲקָרָה בְּאַרְצֶךָ[עו].

יב.

וְעַל פִּי זֶה יֵשׁ לְהוֹסִיף בֵּאוּר בְּמַה שֶּׁנֶּאֱמַר אֶת מִסְפַּר יָמֶיךָ אֲמַלֵּא, אֲמַלֵּא דַיְקָא, שֶׁזֶּהוּ עִנְיָן שֶׁבָּא מִלְמַעְלָה דַוְקָא (נוֹסָף עַל הַהִתְבּוֹנְנוּת דְּהָאָדָם בְּמִסְפַּר הַיָּמִים שֶׁנִּקְצְבוּ לוֹ), וּבָזֶה גוּפָא בִּלְשׁוֹן נוֹכֵחַ, עַל יְדֵי שְׁלִישִׁי הַמְדַבֵּר, בְּחִינַת עַצְמוּת וּמַהוּת אֵין סוֹף בָּרוּךְ הוּא שֶׁלְמַעְלָה מֵהִשְׁתַּלְשְׁלוּת (כַּנַ״ל).

וְהָעִנְיָן בָּזֶה, שֶׁגַּם אִם יֵשׁ אֵיזֶה פְּגַם וְחִסָּרוֹן בְּמִסְפַּר הַיָּמִים דַּעֲבוֹדַת הָאָדָם, שֶׁהָיוּ אֶצְלוֹ יָמִים שֶׁבָּהֶם לֹא מִלֵּא אֶת שְׁלִיחוּתוֹ, אוֹ אֲפִילוּ יָמִים שֶׁבָּהֶם עָשָׂה גַּם עִנְיָנִים בִּלְתִּי־רְצוּיִים כו׳, הֲרֵי מִצַּד בְּחִינַת שְׁלִישִׁי הַמְדַבֵּר שֶׁלְמַעְלָה מֵהִשְׁתַּלְשְׁלוּת, שֶׁשָּׁם לֹא שַׁיָּךְ עִנְיָן שֶׁל פְּגַם, מִתְמַלֵּא מִסְפַּר הַיָּמִים הַקָּצוּב לוֹ, וְעוֹד יוֹתֵר מִכְּפִי הַקָּצוּב כו׳, שֶׁכָּל הַיָּמִים נַעֲשִׂים מְלֵאִים[עז], וְלֹא רַק יָמִים מְלֵאִים, אֶלָּא גַּם יָמִים מְאִירִים, שֶׁזֶּהוּ הַדִּיּוּק דְּמִסְפַּר יָמֶיךָ[עח],

---

122. Regarding the following, see *Torah Or*, *Mishpatim* 79c; *Torat Chaim*, ibid., p. 440a; *Or Hatorah*, ibid., p. 1262.

123. Psalms 19:2.

shine and sparkle.[124] The word *mispar* is also related to a sapphire stone (*even sapir*), related to the Hebrew word *sapirut*, meaning brilliance and luminosity.

13.

ERADICATING DISEASE

This is also the meaning of the verse, *And I will remove illness from your midst*, which is written in the first person—i.e., the Narrator of the Torah is speaking.

The illness—regarding which the verse states, *I will remove illness*—refers to the disease that remains in existence even after *you...serve the L-rd your G-d*, and after *He...blesses your bread and your water. Your bread and your water* refer to the written and oral parts of Torah, respectively.[125] Alternatively, they refer to Torah and *mitzvot*,[126] regarding which the verse states *He shall bless your bread and your water*—that even the service of G-d through performing Torah and *mitzvot* are dependent upon the blessing that emanates from the name *Havaya*.

Even at such a state [i.e., at the level of G-d's name *Havaya*], there is still a possibility for disease. There is therefore a need for *And I will remove illness*, specifically by way of the Narrator of the Torah: *Atzmut*.

ROOT OF ALL DISEASE

The illness[127] that the verse refers to is unqualified illness [without specific description], referring to the root of all illness—the concept of self-consciousness that is a result of the sin of the tree of knowledge.[128]

---

124. See *Zohar* II:136b.

125. Torah provides sustenance to the soul as do bread and water to the body, for the words of Torah unite the soul with G-d, giving life to the soul from the source of life. The Oral Torah corresponds to water, for the mutability of water describes the Oral Law's varied forms of interpretation, whereas the Written Law, like bread, is fixed and solid. For alternative Kabbalistic comparisons, see *Maamarei Admur Hazaken 5568*, ibid.; *Or Ha-*

מִסְפַּר מִלְּשׁוֹן[עט] הַשָּׁמַיִם מְסַפְּרִים פֵּרוּשׁ דִּמְנַהֲרִין וּמְנַצְּצִין[פ], וּמִלְּשׁוֹן אֶבֶן סַפִּיר, שֶׁהוּא לְשׁוֹן סַפִּירוּת וּבְהִירוּת.

יג.

וְזֶהוּ גַּם מַה שֶּׁנֶּאֱמַר וַהֲסִירוֹתִי מַחֲלָה מִקִּרְבֶּךָ בִּלְשׁוֹן נוֹכֵחַ, כִּשְׁלִישִׁי הַמְדַבֵּר.

דְּהִנֵּה, הַמַּחֲלָה שֶׁעָלֶיהָ נֶאֱמַר וַהֲסִירוֹתִי גו׳, הִיא מַחֲלָה כָּזוֹ שֶׁיְּכוֹלָה לִהְיוֹת גַּם כַּאֲשֶׁר וַעֲבַדְתֶּם אֵת הוי׳ אֱלֹקֵיכֶם, וְגַם כַּאֲשֶׁר וּבֵרַךְ אֶת לַחְמְךָ וּמֵימֶיךָ, דְּלַחְמְךָ וּמֵימֶיךָ קָאֵי עַל תּוֹרָה שֶׁבִּכְתָב וְתוֹרָה שֶׁבְּעַל פֶּה[פא], אוֹ תּוֹרָה וּמִצְווֹת[פב], וְעַל זֶה נֶאֱמַר וּבֵרַךְ אֶת לַחְמְךָ וּמֵימֶיךָ, שֶׁהָעֲבוֹדָה בְּתוֹרָה וּמִצְווֹת הִיא מִצַּד הַבְּרָכָה דְּשֵׁם הוי׳,

וְגַם אָז עֲדַיִן יְכוֹלָה לִהְיוֹת מַחֲלָה, וְצָרִיךְ לִהְיוֹת וַהֲסִירוֹתִי מַחֲלָה גו׳ עַל יְדֵי שְׁלִישִׁי הַמְדַבֵּר דַּוְקָא.

וְהָעִנְיָן בָּזֶה[פג], שֶׁמַּחֲלָה שֶׁנֶּאֶמְרָה כַּאן, מַחֲלָה סְתָם, הִיא הַשֹּׁרֶשׁ לְכָל הַמַּחֲלוֹת, וְהִיא הָעִנְיָן דְּהֶרְגֵּשׁ עַצְמוֹ שֶׁבָּא בְּסִבַּת חֵטְא עֵץ הַדַּעַת[פד],

---

torah, ibid., pp. 1255 ff.; 1227; 1235.

126. See *Torat Chaim*, ibid., 440a ff.

127. Regarding the following—see *Torah Or, Mishpatim* 79c-d; *Torat Chaim*, ibid., 440a ff.; *Or Hatorah*, ibid., p. 1262; *Maamarei Admur Hazaken 5568*, p. 410 ff.; *Or Hatorah*, ibid., p. 1211 ff.; p. 1225 ff.; p. 1235 ff.

128. See *Torah Or*, ibid., 79c; *Torat Chaim*, ibid., 440b ff. [302d—ed. 2003]. *Or Hatorah*, ibid., p. 1262.

SIN OF KNOWLEDGE

Before the sin, there were no feelings of self-consciousness, as the verse states, And *they were both [unclothed, man and his wife,] and were not ashamed.*[129] The sin introduced self-consciousness, as the verse states, and *the woman saw that the tree was good for food.*[130]

This is why, even after *You serve the L-rd your G-d and He blesses your bread and your water*, there could still be (and there still is) illness. The sin of the Tree of Knowledge had an effect on everyone, even the righteous—and even the completely righteous, as our Sages state, "Four died through the serpent's machinations,"[131] referring to the greatest and most righteous men who died only because of the sin of the Tree of Knowledge.

"HE WHO LOVES"

Hence, even the completely righteous are subject to self-consciousness. As is known,[132] even a completely righteous person who serves G-d out of awe and love in delight[133] is not completely selfless, but remains a distinct entity who is in awe of G-d and loves Him—"there is an entity who loves." He does not attain the level of cleaving to G-d, which was the level of his soul before it descended to the world below. Certainly, and to an even greater degree, *beinonim* [lit., average people] and those of an even lower caliber [i.e., the wicked] are self-conscious.

A person cannot heal the disease of self-consciousness on his own, but only through eliciting the highest degree of G-dliness. Regarding this the verse specifically states, *And I*

---

129. Genesis 2:25.

130. Ibid., 3:6. After Eve ate from the Tree of Knowledge, she developed a self-conscious perspective, divorced from the G-dly perspective to which she was previously accustomed.

131. *Shabbat* 55b; *Bava Batra* 17a. This was said regarding Benjamin (son of Jacob), Amram (father of Moses), Jesse (father of David), and Chileab (son of David). The purpose of death is to remove impure or evil aspects of the person that are not eternal. The aforementioned righteous

כַּיָּדוּעַ שֶׁקֹּדֶם הַחֵטְא לֹא הָיָה הָעִנְיָן דְּהֶרְגֵּשׁ עַצְמוֹ, וּכְמוֹ שֶׁכָּתוּב[פה] וַיִּהְיוּ שְׁנֵיהֶם גו׳ וְלֹא יִתְבּוֹשָׁשׁוּ, וְעִנְיַן הַחֵטְא הוּא שֶׁנַּעֲשָׂה הֶרְגֵּשׁ עַצְמוֹ, כְּמוֹ שֶׁכָּתוּב[פו] וַתֵּרֶא הָאִשָּׁה כִּי טוֹב הָעֵץ לְמַאֲכָל גו׳.

וְזֶהוּ שֶׁגַּם כַּאֲשֶׁר וַעֲבַדְתֶּם אֵת הוי׳ אֱלֹקֵיכֶם וּבֵרַךְ אֶת לַחְמְךָ וְאֶת מֵימֶיךָ יָכוֹל לִהְיוֹת (וְיֶשְׁנוֹ) עִנְיַן הַמַּחֲלָה, שֶׁהוּא עִנְיַן הֶרְגֵּשׁ עַצְמוֹ, כֵּיוָן שֶׁחֵטְא עֵץ הַדַּעַת פָּעַל עַל כֻּלָּם, גַּם עַל צַדִּיקִים, וְגַם עַל צַדִּיקִים גְּמוּרִים, וּכְמַאֲמַר רַזַ״ל[פז] ד׳ מֵתוּ בְּעֶטְיוֹ שֶׁל נָחָשׁ, שֶׁהֵם צַדִּיקִים הַיּוֹתֵר גְּדוֹלִים, שֶׁסִּבַּת מִיתָתָם אֵינָהּ אֶלָּא בִּגְלַל חֵטְא עֵץ הַדַּעַת,

וְלָכֵן, גַּם בְּצַדִּיקִים גְּמוּרִים שַׁיָּךְ הָעִנְיָן דְּהֶרְגֵּשׁ עַצְמוֹ, וְכַיָּדוּעַ[פח] שֶׁאֲפִילוּ צַדִּיק גָּמוּר עוֹבֵד ה׳ בְּיִרְאָה וְאַהֲבָה בְּתַעֲנוּגִים, אֵינוֹ בָּטֵל בִּמְצִיאוּת לְגַמְרֵי אֶלָּא הוּא דָּבָר בִּפְנֵי עַצְמוֹ יְרֵא ה׳ וְאוֹהֲבוֹ, יֵשׁ מִי שֶׁאוֹהֵב, וְלֹא יַגִּיעַ לְמַעֲלַת דְּבֵקוּתוֹ בַּה׳ כְּמוֹ שֶׁהָיְתָה נִשְׁמָתוֹ קֹדֶם יְרִידָתָהּ לְמַטָּה. וְעַל אַחַת כַּמָּה וְכַמָּה בְּנוֹגֵעַ לְבֵינוֹנִים וְאֵלֶּה שֶׁלְּמַטָּה מִזֶּה, שֶׁאֶצְלָם בְּוַדַּאי יֶשְׁנוֹ הָעִנְיָן דְּהֶרְגֵּשׁ עַצְמוֹ.

וַהֲסָרַת הַמַּחֲלָה דְּהֶרְגֵּשׁ עַצְמוֹ אֵינָהּ יְכוֹלָה לִהְיוֹת עַל יְדֵי עֲבוֹדַת הָאָדָם בְּכֹחַ עַצְמוֹ, כִּי אִם עַל יְדֵי הַמְשָׁכָה נַעֲלֵית בְּיוֹתֵר, וְעַל זֶה נֶאֱמַר וַהֲסִירוֹתִי דַּיְקָא,

---

individuals were in their own right perfect and not deserving of death. Only because of the sin of the Tree of Knowledge (brought about by the serpent's evil machinations) did evil and self-consciousness become inborn into humankind and create the necessity for even the perfectly righteous to undergo death. See also *Likkutei Sichot*, vol. 24, p. 132 ff.

132. See also *Tanya*, ch. 35 (44a ff.); ch. 37 (48a); *Likkutei Torah*, *Balak* 74a.

133. Song of Songs 7:7.

will remove, in the first person, referring to the quintessence of the Infinite, blessed be He[134]—as mentioned earlier.

14.

MATERIALIZED BLESSINGS

Everything mentioned above will also become manifest in the physical. [There will be] abundant livelihood (concerning which the verse states, *And He shall bless your bread and your water*), health (concerning which the verse states, *And I will remove illness from your midst*, and furthermore, *The number of your days I will fill*[135]), and children (concerning which the verse states *None shall miscarry or be barren, in your land)*.

All of this is in preparation for entering the land [of Israel], (regarding which the subsequent verses in the Torah speak[136]). So shall it be for us speedily in our days with the coming of the righteous *Moshiach*.[137]

134. Self-consciousness is a manifestation of ego, giving recognition to a presence other than *atzmut*. Only when a complete realization of *atzmut*'s presence dawns upon the person can he completely escape self-consciousness.

בִּלְשׁוֹן נוֹכֵחַ, שֶׁקָּאֵי עַל עַצְמוּת וּמַהוּת אֵין סוֹף בָּרוּךְ הוּא כַּנַּ"ל.

יד.

וְכָל עִנְיָנִים אֵלֶּה נִמְשָׁכִים גַּם בְּגַשְׁמִיּוּת, הֵן בַּנּוֹגֵעַ לִמְזוֹנָא רְוִיחָא, שֶׁעַל זֶה נֶאֱמַר וּבֵרַךְ אֶת לַחְמְךָ וְאֶת מֵימֶיךָ, הֵן בַּנּוֹגֵעַ לְחַיֵּי, שֶׁעַל זֶה נֶאֱמַר וַהֲסִירוֹתִי מַחֲלָה מִקִּרְבֶּךָ, וּמוֹסִיף אֶת מִסְפַּר יָמֶיךָ אֲמַלֵּא, וְהֵן בַּנּוֹגֵעַ לְבָנֵי, שֶׁעַל זֶה נֶאֱמַר לֹא תִהְיֶה מְשַׁכֵּלָה וַעֲקָרָה בְּאַרְצֶךָ.

וְכָל זֶה נַעֲשָׂה הֲכָנָה לְעִנְיַן כְּנִיסַת הָאָרֶץ (שֶׁעַל זֶה מְדֻבָּר בְּהֶמְשֵׁךְ הַכְּתוּבִים[פט]), כֵּן תִּהְיֶה לָנוּ בִּמְהֵרָה בְיָמֵינוּ עַל יְדֵי מָשִׁיחַ צִדְקֵנוּ[צ].

---

135. That is, blessings for longevity as well as blessings for health (see ch. 1).

136. Verses 27-31.

137. An original, lengthier closing is missing from this transcript.

HEBREW NOTES

הערות לד״ה לא תהיה משכלה

א) פרשתנו כג, כו. — חלק מהמאמר שולב ונדפס בלקו״ש חט״ז ע׳ 271 ואילך.
ב) שם, כה.
ג) ראה ד״ה לא תהי׳ משכלה בתורת חיים פרשתנו תמ, א [בהוצאה החדשה — שב, ג]. אוה״ת פרשתנו ע׳ א׳רמח.
ד) ראה תורת חיים שם.
ה) מקץ מג, יד. וראה פרש״י תולדות כז, מה.
ו) ראה לקו״ת סוכות פ, סע״ד. ובכ״מ.
ז) ראה מו״ק כח, א. וראה אוה״ת וירא (כרך ד) תשנה, ב ואילך. ביאוה״ז להצ״צ ח״א ע׳ מד ואילך. ח״ב ע׳ תרלז ואילך. ועוד.
ח) בהבא לקמן — ראה ד״ה ועבדתם את ה״א במאמרי אדה״ז תקס״ח ח״א ע׳ תב; אוה״ת פרשתנו ע׳ א׳קצח ואילך. ע׳ א׳ריט ואילך; סה״מ תרס״ב ע׳ רעג ואילך.
ט) תקו״ז בהקדמה (יז, ב). ובכ״מ.
י) ראה גם ד״ה לא תהי׳ משכלה בתו״א פרשתנו עח, סע״ד. אוה״ת שם ע׳ א׳רנה.
יא) ראה עבודת הקודש בהקדמה. שם ח״ב (חלק העבודה) פ״ג. הובא בשל״ה שער הגדול כט, ב ואילך. אוה״ת פרשתנו ע׳ א׳ריט ואילך. סה״מ תרס״ב שם. וראה גם ד״ה זאת תורת העולה תרע״ח. תש״מ. ובכ״מ.
יב) ב״ר רפמ״ד. תנחומא שמיני ח.
יג) איוב לה, ו־ז.
יד) איכ״ר פ״א, לג. שבת פט, א. וראה גם לקו״ת שלח לט, ב ואילך. מ, א. אוה״ת שלח ע׳ תסט ואילך. ע׳ תעב. ע׳ תעט. אוה״ת נ״ך ח״א ע׳ תרעט. ובכ״מ.
טו) שלח יד, יז.
טז) איכ״ר שם. ועוד.
יז) האזינו לב, יח.
יח) בכל הבא לקמן — ראה ד״ה צאינה וראינה עזר״ת (סה״מ עזר״ת ס״ע קצה ואילך).
יט) סה״מ עזר״ת שם. ובכ״מ.
כ) ח״ב שם. הובא בשל״ה שם.
כא) ראה זח״א לא, ריש ע״ב. תו״ח בראשית א, א. סידור (עם דא״ח) שה, ד. ובכ״מ.
כב) בהבא לקמן — ראה סה״מ עזר״ת שם ע׳ ר ואילך.
כג) ראה סה״מ עזר״ת שם ע׳ קצו ואילך. ועוד.
כד) ראה ספר הערכים־חב״ד ח״ד ערך אורות דספירות ביחס לכלים. וש״נ.
כה) עץ חיים שער מב (שער דרושי אבי״ע) פ״א. הובא בסה״מ עזר״ת שם.
כו) לך לך יב, ח. ועוד. וראה לקו״ת אמור לא, ד. ד״ה באתי לגני תשמ״ח פ״ז ואילך (תו״מ סה״מ שבט ע׳ תז ואילך). ובכ״מ.
כז) אוה״ת פרשתנו ע׳ א׳ריט. ע׳ א׳רלט. סה״מ תרס״ב שם ע׳ ערב.
כח) זח״ג רנז, ב (ברע״מ). פרדס שער א (שער עשר ולא תשע) פ״ט. תניא שעהיוה״א פ״ז (פב, א).
כט) פרדס שם. תניא שעהיוה״א רפ״ד. וראה זהר שם.

ל) ראה עטרת ראש שער ר״ה פרק ד. ועוד.

לא) הושע ו, ב.

לב) ראה אוה״ת פרשתנו ע׳ א׳ריט. סה״מ תרס״ב שם ע׳ רפד. לקו״ת דרושים לר״ה סד, א. וראה אוה״ת פרשתנו ע׳ א׳רנא. תו״ח פרשתנו תלח, ב [שא, ג] ואילך.

לג) ראה תניא פל״ב.

לד) ראה גם ד״ה בשעה שהקדימו שנה זו (תו״מ סה״מ תשי״ב ע׳ שי).

לה) בשלח טו, כו.

לו) וראה לקמן בסוף המאמר.

לז) תניא פמ״א (נו, א). קונטרס העבודה פרק ב.

לח) תניא שם (נז, א). וראה לקו״ש ח״ז ע׳ 183.

לט) ראה קידושין כג, ב וברשב״א שם.

מ) גיטין יג, א. וש״נ. וראה ד״ה ואלה המשפטים תשל״ח פ״ה ואילך (תו״מ סה״מ אדר ע׳ י ואילך). וש״נ.

מא) ראה קונטרס העבודה שם (ע׳ 13).

מב) ראה קונטרס העבודה פרק א (ע׳ 4).

מג) ריש הל׳ תפלה.

מד) עקב יא, יג.

מה) תענית ב, סע״א.

מו) ראה זח״ב נה, ב. זח״ג רסז, א. לקו״ת שלח מב, ג. קונטרס העבודה פ״א. פ״ג ואילך. וראה ספר הערכים־חב״ד כרך א ערך אהבת ה׳ ס״ה. ס״ט. וש״נ.

מז) בהבא לקמן — ראה קונטרס העבודה פ״א־ג.

מח) קונטרס העבודה שם (ע׳ 4). תו״א תרומה עט, סע״ד (וראה הערת כ״ק אדמו״ר שליט״א בסה״מ תש״ט ע׳ 79). וראה גם תו״א פרשתנו עט, ב. תו״ח שם תלד, ב [חצר, סע״ג ואילך]. מאמרי אדה״ז תקס״ח שם ע׳ תב. אוה״ת פרשתנו שם ע׳ א׳קצח. ועוד.

מט) תניא פי״ג (יח, ריש ע״ב).

נ) תניא פל״ז (מח, ב) מע״ח שער כ״ו פ״א.

נא) תו״א בראשית ה, ב. פרשתנו עו, א. לקו״ת ויקרא ב, ד. ובכ״מ.

נב) שמצויין בהערה מז.

נג) בהבא לקמן — ראה תו״א פרשתנו עט, א ואילך. תו״ח שם תלא, ב [רצו, ד] ואילך. אוה״ת שם ע׳ א׳רנו ואילך. סה״מ תרצ״ב ע׳ רכב.

נד) ראה תניא פ״ג. ובכ״מ.

נה) ראה תו״א שם. תו״ח שם תלב, א [רצז, א] ואילך. אוה״ת שם.

נו) ראה ב״ר פמ״ז, ב. פנ״ג, ה. פס״ג, ה. הובא באור החיים וירא כא, ב.

נז) יבמות סד, ריש ע״ב.

נז) ברכות מ, א.

נט) תניא פ״ח (יג, רע״א). מזח״ג רנג, א. רעז, א.

ס) ראה גם לקו״ת שה״ש לט, ד ואילך. המשך כל הנהנה תרנ״ב (סה״מ תרנ״ב ע׳ קל). המשך שמח תשמח תרנ״ז (סה״מ תרנ״ז ע׳ קעט). ובכ״מ.

סא) תהלים צז, יא.

סב) ראה סה״מ תש״ג ע׳ 47. ועוד.

סג) ראה תו״ח בשלח קסא, ב [פ׳ בא קכט, א] ואילך. ועוד.

סד) משלי יב, יט. וראה אוה״ת פרשתנו שם ע׳ א׳רסה.

סה) תהלים צט, ד.

סו) ראה תו״א שם עט, א. תו״ח פרשתנו תלא, ב [רצו, ד]. אוה״ת שם ע׳ א׳רנה.

סז) ראה תו״א שם עח, סע״ד. תו״ח שם תלא, א [רצו, ד]. אוה״ת שם ריש ע׳ א׳רנה.

סח) ב״ר פ״ה, ח ובמתנות כהונה שם.

סט) בהבא לקמן — ראה תו״א פרשתנו עט, סע״ב ואילך. תו״ח שם תלז, א ואילך. אוה״ת שם ע׳ א׳רסא ואילך. סה״מ תרצ״ב ע׳ רכג.

ע) תהלים קלט, טז. וראה זח״א רכד, א. תו״א שם. תו״ח שם תלז, ב ואילך. אוה״ת שם. וראה גם ד״ה וידבר גו׳ וארא שנה זו (תו״מ סה״מ תשי״ב ע׳ קצז). ד״ה ואברהם זקן תשל״ח (תו״מ סה״מ חשון ע׳ שז ואילך). וש״נ.

עא) ברכות כח, ב.

עב) ראה עוד ביאורים במאמרי אדה״ז הקצרים ע׳ שט. ועם הגהות — אוה״ת פינחס ע׳ א׳נט ואילך. סה״מ תרכ״ו ע׳ קעא ואילך. תרמ״ו ע׳ יד ואילך. תרצ״ו ע׳ 50 ואילך.

עג) להעיר מקיצורים והערות לתניא ע׳ מז.

עד) להעיר מד״ה ויקח ה״א שנה זו (תו״מ סה״מ תשי״ב ע׳ קנח). ד״ה בראשית ברא תשי״ג (תו״מ סה״מ תשי״ג ע׳ כה ואילך).

עה) בחלק זה דהמאמר פרץ כ״ק אדמו״ר שליט״א בבכי רב, והניח ראשו הק׳ על השולחן, ורק לאחרי משך זמן המשיך באמירת המאמר (המו״ל).

עו) חסר קצת (המו״ל).

עז) ראה תו״ח שם תלט, ב ואילך. וראה אוה״ת פרשתנו ע׳ א׳רסו. שם (כרך ז) ס״ע ב׳תשלא.

עח) בהבא לקמן — ראה תו״א פרשתנו עט, ג. תו״ח שם תמ, רע״א. אוה״ת שם ע׳ א׳רסב.

עט) תהלים יט, ב.

פ) ראה זח״ב קלו, ב.

פא) מאמרי אדה״ז תקס״ח שם. אוה״ת שם ע׳ א׳רכה ואילך. ע׳ א׳רכז. ע׳ א׳רלה.

פב) תו״ח שם תמ, סע״א ואילך.

פג) בהבא לקמן — ראה תו״א פרשתנו עט, ג־ד. תו״ח שם תמ, א ואילך. אוה״ת שם ע׳ א׳רסב. מאמרי אדה״ז תקס״ח שם ס״ע תי ואילך. אוה״ת שם ס״ע א׳ריא ואילך. ע׳ א׳רכה ואילך. ע׳ א׳רלה ואילך.

פד) ראה תו״א שם עט, ד. תו״ח שם תמ, ב ואילך. אוה״ת שם ע׳ א׳רסב. ועוד.

פה) בראשית ב, כה.

פו) שם ג, ו.

פז) שבת נה, ב. ב״ב יז, א. וראה גם לקו״ש חכ״ד ע׳ 132 ואילך.

פח) ראה גם תניא פל״ה (מד, סע״א ואילך). פל״ז (מח, סע״א).

פט) בפסוקים כז־לא.

צ) חסר אריכות הדברים בסיום המאמר (המו״ל).

BIBLIOGRAPHY

BIBLIOGRAPHY

Ateret Rosh: Chasidic exposition of Rosh Hashanah, Yom Kippur, the Ten Days of Penitence and Shabbat Shuvah by Rabbi DovBer, second Lubavitcher Rebbe. (Kopust, 1821; Shanghai, 1947. Revised Edition, Kehot, Brooklyn, 1989)

Avodat Hakodesh: Kabbalistic work by Rabbi Meir ibn Gabbai of Spain and Egypt (16th century), one of the first and foremost systematists of the Kabbalah. Completed in 1531.

Avot: "Ethics of the Fathers." Talmudic tractate discussing moral and ethical teachings.

Baal Shem Tov Al HaTorah: Chasidic insights on the Torah and festivals collected from the works of disciples of R. Yisrael Baal Shem Tov (1698-1760), by Rabbi Shimon Menachem Mendel Wednik. (Lodz, 1938)

Bava Batra: Talmudic tractate dealing with the laws of ownership of real property, inheritance, and documents.

Berachot: Talmudic tractate addressing the laws of reading the Shema, prayer, and blessings.

Bereshit Bara 5713: Chasidic Discourse delivered by the Lubavitcher Rebbe, R. Menachem M. Schneerson, on Shabbat Bereshit, 5713 (1952).

Bereshit Rabbah: See *Midrash Rabbah.*

Biurei Hazohar: Kabbalistic and Chasidic Discourses explaining the *Zohar* and the *Tikkunei Zohar* by R. Menachem Mendel Schneersohn, third Lubavitcher Rebbe, the "Tzemach Tzedek."

B'shaah Shehikdumu 5712: Chasidic Discourse delivered by the Lubavitcher Rebbe, R. Menachem M. Schneerson, on the second day of Shavuot, 5712 (1952).

Eichah Rabbah: See *Midrash Rabbah.*

Eitz Chaim: A compilation of the Arizal's Kabbalistic teachings, by his primary disciple and exponent, Rabbi Chaim Vital (1543-1620).

Feminine Faith: English translation of *Lehavin Inyan Rosh Chodesh*, delivered by the fourth Lubavitcher Rebbe, R. Shmuel Schneersohn, on Shabbat Noach, Rosh Chodesh Marcheshvan, 5640 (1879). (Kehot, 2009)

Gittin: Talmudic tractate discussing the laws of divorce.

Hayom Yom: Anthology of aphorisms and customs arranged according to the days of the year; assembled by the Lubavitcher Rebbe, Rabbi Menachem M. Schneerson, from the talks and writings of his father-in-law, Rabbi Yosef Y. Schneersohn. (Kehot, 1943)

Iggeret Hakodesh: Fourth part of *Tanya* by R. Schneur Zalman of Liadi; discussing such topics as charity, prayer, and the like; thirty-two epistles.

Kiddushin: Talmudic tractate discussing the laws of marriage.

Kitzurim V'he'orot L'Tanya: "Summaries and comments to Tanya" by R. Menachem Mendel Schneersohn, third Lubavitcher Rebbe, the "Tzemach Tzedek." Includes supplements by a number of the successive Lubavitcher Rebbes. (Kehot, 1948; 1989)

Kuntres Ha'avodah: Short, self-contained Chasidic work explaining prayer—the service of the heart—and the role and dynamics of contemplation before and during prayer. The intellectual concepts discussed are meant to form a basis for meditation that will lead to the love and fear of G-d. (Brooklyn, 1946)

Likkutei Sichot: Talks delivered and edited by the Lubavitcher Rebbe, Rabbi Menachem M. Schneerson. (Thirty-nine vol., Kehot, 1962-2001).

Likkutei Torah: Chasidic discourses elucidating major themes of Leviticus, Numbers, Deuteronomy, Song of Songs, Pesach, Shavuot, the High Holidays and Sukkot by R. Schneur Zalman of Liadi. First published by his grandson R. Menachem Mendel Schneersohn, third Lubavitcher Rebbe, the "Tzemach Tzedek," in 5608 (1848).

Maamarei Amdur Hazaken 5568: Discourses delivered by Rabbi Schneur Zalman of Liadi during the year 5568 (1807-8).

Maamarei Admor Hazaken Haktzarim: Short discourses delivered by Rabbi Schneur Zalman of Liadi on various topics.

Matnot Kehunah: A commentary appearing in nearly every edition of the *Midrash*, by R. Yissachar Naftali HaKohen Ashkenazi (16th-17th Century); student of R. Moshe Isserles (Rama).

Midrash Rabbah: A major collection of homilies and commentaries on the Torah, attributed to R. Oshaya Rabbah (circa. 3rd century); some place it as a work of the early Gaonic period.

Moed Katan: Talmudic tractate discussing the laws of *Chol Hamoed*, the intermediary days of Pesach and Sukkot.

Mystical Concepts in Chassidism: Guide to the intricate concepts of Jewish mysticism found in Chabad Chasidic philosophy. Authored by Rabbi J. Immanuel Schochet (Kehot, 1988). (Eng.)

Or Hachaim: Popular Commentary on the Torah by R. Chaim ibn Attar (1696-1743). First published in Venice, 1742.

Or Hatorah: Chasidic discourses on Scripture by R. Menachem Mendel Schneersohn, third Lubavitcher Rebbe, the "Tzemach Tzedek." (Berditchev, 1913; Brooklyn, NY, 1950 and on)

Overcoming Folly: English translation of *Kuntres Umaayan*, an ethical treatise by R. Shalom DovBer Schneersohn, fifth Lubavitcher Rebbe. (Brooklyn, 2006. Hebrew: Brooklyn, 1943)

Pardes (Pardes Rimonim): Kabbalistic work by R. Moshe Cordovero (Ramak) of Safed (1522-1570), leader of a prominent Kabbalistic school in Safed.

The Path to Selflessness: English translation of *Yehudah Atah*, a Chasidic discourse delivered by the Lubavitcher Rebbe, R. Menachem M. Schneerson, on the fast of the Tenth of Tevet, 5738 (1977). (Kehot, 2009)

Sefer HaArachim—Chabad: Encyclopedia of topics discussed in Chasidus, gathered from the writings of seven generations of Chabad Rebbes (Brooklyn, 1970 and on)

Sefer Hamaamarim 5643-5680: Set of Chasidic discourses delivered by Rabbi Shalom DovBer Schneersohn, fifth Lubavitcher Rebbe, between 5643-5680 (1883-1920), the years of his leadership; twenty-five volumes.

Sefer Hamaamarim 5680-5710: Set of Chasidic discourses delivered by Rabbi Yosef Yitzchak Schneersohn, sixth Lubavitcher Rebbe, between 5680-5710 (1920-1950), the years of his leadership; nineteen volumes.

Sefer Hamaamarim 5740: Chasidic discourses delivered by the Lubavitcher Rebbe, Rabbi Menachem M. Schneerson, during 5740 (1979-1980).

Sefer Hamaamarim Melukat: Chasidic discourses delivered and edited by the Lubavitcher Rebbe, Rabbi Menachem M. Schneerson, during the course of his leadership 5711-5752 (1951-1992). (Six vol., Kehot, 1987-1992; new edition, 2002, four vol.)

Shaar Hayichud v'haEmunah: Second part of *Tanya* by R. Schneur Zalman of Liadi; explores the doctrines of Divine Unity, Providence and faith; twelve chapters.

Shabbat: Talmudic tractate discussing the laws of Shabbat.

Shelah: Monumental work by R. Yeshayah Horowitz, (1558-1628), chief rabbi of Prague. Also known by its acronym, *Shelah*, it contains explanations and commentaries on the profound aspects of the Torah, *mitzvot*, the festivals, Jewish customs and the fundamental beliefs of Judaism, including basic instruction in Kabbalah. First published in Amsterdam, 1648.

Siddur im Dach: Lit., "Siddur with Chasidus." Also known as *Seder Tefillot Mikol Hashanah* (The Order of the Prayers of the Entire Year), this is a prayer book containing rulings and Chasidic discourses pertaining to the prayers by Rabbi Schneur Zalman of Liadi.

Taanit: Talmudic tractate discussing fast days.

Tanchuma: Early *Midrash* on the Torah, attributed to R. Tanchuma bar Abba. (Constantinople, 1522)

Tanya: Philosophical *magnum opus* by Rabbi Schneur Zalman of Liadi, in which the principles of Chabad are expounded. The name is derived from the initial word of this work. Also called *Likkutei Amarim*. See also *Iggeret Hakodesh* and *Shaar Hayichud v'haEmunah*.

Targum Yerushalmi: Ancient Aramaic translation of the Torah, usually appearing alongside the *Targum Yonatan* and probably written around the same time or somewhat earlier.

Tikkunim; Tikkunei Zohar: A work of seventy chapters on the first word of the Torah, by the school of Rabbi Shimon bar Yochai (c. 120 C.E.). First printed in Mantua, 1558, *Tikkunei Zohar* contains some of the most important discussions in *Kabbalah*, and is essential for understanding the *Zohar*.

Torah Or: Chasidic discourses elucidating major themes of Genesis, Exodus, Chanukah, and Purim by Rabbi Schneur Zalman of Liadi. First published by his grandson Rabbi Menachem Mendel Schneersohn, third Lubavitcher Rebbe, the "Tzemach Tzedek," in 5597 (1837).

Torat Chaim: Chasidic discourses elucidating major themes of Genesis, Exodus, Chanukah, and Purim by Rabbi Dov-Ber of Lubavitch. (Kopust, 1886; Kehot, Brooklyn, 1974; revised edition, 2003)

Torat Shmuel—Sefer 5626: Chasidic discourses delivered by Rabbi Shmuel Schneersohn, fourth Lubavitcher Rebbe, during the year 5626 (1865-6).

Transforming the Inner Self: English translation of *Adam Ki Yakriv*, a Chasidic discourse delivered by Rabbi Schneur Zalman of Liadi, on Shabbat Vayikra, 5572 (1812). (Kehot, 2004)

True Existence: English translation of *Mi Chamocha, 5629*, a Chasidic discourse delivered by R. Shmuel Schneersohn, fourth Lubavitcher Rebbe, on Shabbat Yitro and Shabbat Shemini, 5629 (1869). (Kehot, 2002)

V'Avraham Zaken 5738: Chasidic Discourse delivered by the Lubavitcher Rebbe, R. Menachem M. Schneerson, at the close of Shabbat Chayei Sara, 5738 (1977).

Vayedaber...Va'erah 5712: Chasidic Discourse delivered by the Lubavitcher Rebbe, R. Menachem M. Schneerson, on Shabbat Va'era, 5712 (1952).

Vayikach Hashem Elokim 5712: Chasidic Discourse delivered by the Lubavitcher Rebbe, R. Menachem M. Schneerson, on Shabbat Bereshit, 5712 (1951).

Yevamot: Talmudic tractate discussing levirate marriage.

Yom Tov Shel Rosh Hashanah 5666: Series of discourses delivered by Rabbi Shalom DovBer Schneersohn, fifth Lubavitcher Rebbe, during the years 5666-7 (1905-7), named for its opening words.

Zohar: Basic work of Kabbalah; compiled by Rabbi Shimon Bar Yochai (second century Mishnaic sage); written in Hebrew and Aramaic as a commentary on the Torah.

INDEX

INDEX

N

O

P

S

T

Y

OTHER TITLES IN
THE CHASIDIC HERITAGE SERIES

Rabbi Schneur Zalman of Liadi

THE ETERNAL BOND *from Torah Or*

Translated by Rabbi Ari Sollish

This discourse explores the spiritual significance of *brit milah*, analyzing two dimensions in which our connection with G-d may be realized. For in truth, there are two forms of spiritual circumcision. Initially, man must "circumcise his heart," freeing himself to the best of his ability from his negative, physical drives; ultimately, though, it is G-d who truly liberates man from his material attachment.

JOURNEY OF THE SOUL from *Torah Or*

Translated by Rabbi Ari Sollish

Drawing upon the parallel between Queen Esther's impassioned plea to King Ahasuerus for salvation and the soul's entreaty to G-d for help in its spiritual struggle, this discourse examines the root of the soul's exile, and the dynamics by which it lifts itself from the grip of materialism and ultimately finds a voice with which to express its G-dly yearnings. Includes a brief biography of the author.

TRANSFORMING THE INNER SELF from *Likkutei Torah*

Translated by Rabbi Chaim Zev Citron

This discourse presents a modern-day perspective on the Biblical command to offer animal sacrifices. Rabbi Schneur Zalman teaches that each of us possesses certain character traits that can be seen as "animalistic," or materialistic, in nature, which can lead a person toward a life of material indulgence. Our charge, then, is to "sacrifice" and transform the animal within, to refine our animal traits and utilize them in our pursuit of spiritual perfection.

Rabbi DovBer of Lubavitch

FLAMES from *Shaarei Orah*

Translated by Dr. Naftoli Loewenthal

This discourse focuses on the multiple images of the lamp, the oil, the wick and the different hues of the flame in order to express profound guidance in the Divine service of every individual. Although *Flames* is a Chanukah discourse, at the same time, it presents concepts that are of perennial significance. Includes the first English biography of the author ever published.

Rabbi Menachem Mendel of Lubavitch,
the Tzemach Tzedek

THE MITZVAH TO LOVE YOUR FELLOW AS YOURSELF

from *Derech Mitzvotecha*

Translated by Rabbis Nissan Mangel and Zalman I. Posner

The discourse discusses the Kabbalistic principle of the "collective soul of the world of *Tikkun*" and explores the essential unity of all souls. The discourse develops the idea that when we connect on a soul level, we can love our fellow as we love ourselves; for in truth, we are all one soul. Includes a brief biography of the author.

Rabbi Shmuel of Lubavitch

TRUE EXISTENCE

Mi Chamocha 5629

Translated by Rabbis Yosef Marcus and Avraham D. Vaisfiche

This discourse revolutionizes the age-old notion of Monotheism, i.e., that there is no other god besides Him. Culling from Talmudic and Midrashic sources, the discourse makes the case that not only is there no other god besides Him, there is nothing besides Him—literally. The only thing that truly exists is G-d. Includes a brief biography of the author.

TRUE EXISTENCE *The Chasidic View of Reality*

A Video-CD with Rabbi Manis Friedman

Venture beyond science and Kabbalah and discover the world of Chasidism. This Video-CD takes the viewer step-by-step through the basic Chasidic and Kabbalistic view of creation and existence. In clear, lucid language, Rabbi Manis Friedman deciphers these esoteric concepts and demonstrates their modern-day applications.

CHANNELING THE DIVINE

Itta B'Midrash Tillim

Edited by Rabbi Avraham D. Vaisfiche

The Bar Mitzvah, the day a Jewish boy turns thirteen, is a turning point in his life. He comes of age, becoming responsible for adherence to the *mitzvot* and fully accountable for his actions—and everyone celebrates. Chabad Chasidim mark this milestone by having the "Bar Mitzvah boy" publicly deliver a discourse, originally delivered by Rabbi Shalom DovBer Schneersohn, fifth Lubavitcher Rebbe, on the occasion of his Bar Mitzvah in 5634 (1873). Its main theme is the cosmic impact of performing the mitzvah of *tefillin*, and the special connection between this mitzvah and the age of Bar Mitzvah.

FEMININE FAITH

L'Havin Inyan Rosh Chodesh, 5640

Translated by Rabbi Shais Taub

When the Jews served the Golden Calf during their sojourn in the wilderness, says the Midrash, the women refused to join them. Feminine Faith traces the roots of the feminine within the supernal-realms, and explores its relationship to women and how it translated into their aversion for unholy and ungodly worship. Why are-women more sensitive than men to G-d's role in earthly events and His mastery over Creation? In this discourse, Rabbi Shmuel Schneersohn, fourth leader of Chabad Lubavitch (1834-1882), explores G-d's unity and immanence in the world, and the innate sensitivity that women posses to spirituality.

Rabbi Shalom DovBer of Lubavitch

YOM TOV SHEL ROSH HASHANAH 5659

Discourse One

Translated by Rabbis Yosef Marcus and Moshe Miller

The discourse explores the attribute of *malchut* and the power of speech while introducing some of the basic concepts of Chasidism and Kabbalah in a relatively easy to follow format. Despite its title and date of inception, the discourse is germane throughout the year. Includes a brief biography of the author.

FORCES IN CREATION

Yom Tov Shel Rosh Hashanah 5659 Discourse Two

Translated by Rabbis Moshe Miller and Shmuel Marcus

A fascinating journey beyond the terrestrial, into the myriad spiritual realms that shape our existence. Rabbi Shalom DovBer systematically traces the origins of earth, Torah and souls, drawing the reader higher and higher into the mystical, cosmic dimensions that lie beyond the here and now, and granting a deeper awareness of who we are at our core.

THE POWER OF RETURN

Yom Tov Shel Rosh Hashanah 5659 Discourse Three

Translated by Rabbi Y. Eliezer Danzinger

This discourse examines the inner workings of *teshuvah*, and explains how it is precisely through making a detailed and honest examination of one's character and spiritual standing—which inevitably leads one to a contrite and broken heart—that allows one to realize his or her essential connection with G-d.

TRACT ON PRAYER

Kuntres HaTefillah

Translated by Rabbi Y. Eliezer Danzinger

Tract on Prayer expounds on the concept of *tefillah*—prayer, as understood in Chabad Chasidic philosophy. Building on the Talmudic dictum that prayer constitutes the "service of the heart," *Tract on Prayer* captures the quintessence of *tefillah* as the vehicle for attaining attachment to G-d. It guides the worshiper in preparing for this divine service of the heart, setting out the role and dynamics of contemplation before and during prayer. *Tract on Prayer* also explores various Kabbalistic and Chasidic concepts.

OVERCOMING FOLLY

Kuntres Umaayan Mibeit Hashem

Translated by Rabbi Zalman I. Posner

In this classis ethico-philosophical work, Rabbi Shalom DovBer weaves Chasidic doctrine, Kabbalah thoughts, Biblical and Talmudic texts and candid insights into human frailties into a document structured and systematic, yet informal and personal—a text for study and meditation.

THE SIMPLE SERVANT

UMikneh Rav 5666

Translated by Rabbi Yosef Marcus

This discourse elaborates upon three types of personalities with distinct approaches to Divine service: 1) The child of G-d, naturally committed; 2) The loyal servant of G-d, motivated by his appreciation of G-d; 3) The simple servant of G-d, driven by his acceptance of the yoke of Heaven. His apathy makes serving G-d difficult. Yet he does his work consistently because he is reaching beyond himself—overcoming his own nature.

THE PRINCIPLES OF EDUCATION AND GUIDANCE

Klalei Hachinuch Vehahadrachah

Translated by Rabbi Y. Eliezer Danzinger

The Principles of Education and Guidance is a compelling treatise that examines the art of educating. In this thought-provoking analysis, Rabbi Yosef Yitzchak teaches how to assess the potential of any pupil, how to objectively evaluate one's own strengths, and how to successfully use reward and punishment—methods that will help one become a more effective educator.

THE FOUR WORLDS

Translated by Rabbis Yosef Marcus and Avraham D. Vaisfiche

Overview by Rabbi J. Immanuel Schochet

At the core of our identity is the desire to be one with our source, and to know the spiritual realities that give our physical life the transcendental importance of the Torah's imperatives. In this letter to a yearning Chasid, the Rebbe explains the mystical worlds of *Atzilut*, *Beriah*, *Yetzirah*, and *Asiyah*.

ONENESS IN CREATION

Kol Hamaarich B'Echad 5690

Translated by Rabbi Y. Eliezer Danzinger

Said by Rabbi Yosef Yitzchak at the close of his 1930 visit to Chicago, this discourse explores the concept of Divine Unity as expressed in the first verse of the *Shema*. The discourse maintains that it is a G-dly force that perpetually sustains all of creation. As such, G-d is one with creation. And it is our study of Torah and performance of the mitzvot that reveals this essential oneness.

CREATION AND REDEMPTION

Hachodesh 5700

Translated by Rabbi Yosef Marcus

Tishrei celebrates Creation, the birth of the world, indicative of the natural order. Nissan commemorates the miraculous Exodus from Egypt, or the supernatural. In human terms, when struggling with the obfuscation of the natural, the key is to recognize the dimension where the limitations of the natural order do not exist. In fact, the physical exists only so that we may demonstrate how it too exposes the Divine truth. And when we recognize this, we can realize the supernatural even within the natural.

THE MAJESTIC BRIDE

Lecha Dodi 5689 / 5714

Translated by Rabbis Ari Sollish and Avraham D. Vaisfiche

Customarily recited by a groom at the Kabbalat Panim reception, *Lecha Dodi* traces the Kabbalistic meaning of the order of the wedding ceremony, when first the guests welcome the groom, and then walk with the groom to welcome the bride, at which point the groom covers the bride's face with the veil. The discourse cites a number of examples and other situations where similar procedures occur, finally applying the reasoning to groom and bride to understand the Kabbalat Panim ceremony and the purpose of marriage.

Rabbi Menachem M. Schneerson,
the Lubavitcher Rebbe

ON THE ESSENCE OF CHASIDUS

Kuntres Inyana Shel Toras Hachasidus

This landmark discourse explores the contribution of Chasidus to a far deeper and expanded understanding of Torah. The Rebbe analyzes the relationship Chasidus has with Kabbalah, the various dimensions of the soul, the concept of Moshiach and the Divine attributes.

GARMENTS OF THE SOUL

Vayishlach Yehoshua 5736

Translated by Rabbi Yosef Marcus

Often what is perceived in this world as secondary is in reality most sublime. What appears to be mundane and inconsequential is often most sacred and crucial. Thus, at their source, the garments of the human, both physical and spiritual, transcend the individual.

THE UNBREAKABLE SOUL

Mayim Rabbim 5738

Translated by Rabbi Ari Sollish

No matter how much one may be inundated with materialism, the flame of the soul burns forever. A discourse that begins with an unequivocal declaration, it speaks to one who finds pleasure in the material world, yet struggles to find spirituality in his or her life.

VICTORY OF LIGHT

Tanu Rabanan Mitzvat Ner Chanukah 5738

Translated by Rabbi Yosef Marcus

Even darkness has a purpose: to be transformed into light. This discourse explains how we can draw strength from the story of Chanukah for our battle with spiritual darkness, so that we, like the Macabees of old, may attain a *Victory of Light.*

THE PATH TO SELFLESSNESS

Yehudah Atah 5738

Translated by Rabbi Shmuel Simpson

Beginning with the words *Yehuda Atah*, the discourse examines the blessing which Yaakov blessed his fourth son, Yehuda, as compared to the blessings he gave his first three sons, Reuven, Shimon and Levi. Yaakov's sons embody distinctive forms of divine service, which correspond to distinct sections of the prayers of Shema and the Amidah. Using these distinctions, the discourse further derives lessons about the bond between the individual Jewish soul and G-d.

ର୍ଗର୍ଗର୍ଗ

NURTURING FAITH

Kuntres Purim Kattan 5752

Translated by Rabbi Yosef Marcus

At its core, this discourse discusses the function of a *nassi*, a Jewish leader, who awakens within every single person the deepest part of the soul. Similar to Moses, the *nassi* inspires the person so that one's most basic faith in G-d leaves the realm of the abstract and becomes real. *Nurturing Faith* will cultivate your bond with the Rebbe's role as the Moses of our generation.

ର୍ଗର୍ଗର୍ଗ

COMING SOON!

STAYING THE COURSE

A collection of discourses by the Chabad Rebbes on the eternal bond between Rebbe and Chasid that continues after the Rebbe's passing.

PADAH BESHALOM 5668

By Rabbi Shalom DovBer of Lubavitch
Translated by Rabbi Zalman Abraham

Dedicated in honor of
the Rebbe's shluchim and shluchos
around the world

And in loving memory of
Mrs. **Chaya Zlata** bas Reb **Yehoshua Geisinsky**
who was dedicated to her community
and to her shlichus

by
Yaakov and **Karen Cohen**
and **family**
Potomac, Maryland

הוצאת ספרים
קה"ת
קרני הוד תורה
ליובאוויטש